Oligopolistic Reaction
and Multinational Enterprise

Oligopolistic Reaction and Multinational Enterprise

Frederick T. Knickerbocker

Lecturer on Business Administration
Harvard University

Division of Research
Graduate School of Business Administration
Harvard University

Boston · 1973

Library of Congress Catalog Card No. 72–94361
ISBN 0–87584–102–3

*This book won the Richard D. Irwin Prize for the
Best Doctoral Dissertation 1971–1972 at the
Harvard Business School*

Printed in the United States of America

Foreword

It has been only a very few years since the term multinational enterprise has been put in general circulation. But multinational enterprises under one name or another have been the subject of politicians' invective, journalists' commentary, and scholars' curiosity for a good many decades. From the beginning of the present century, it was already being widely noted that U.S. enterprises had a high propensity to establish branches and subsidiaries overseas.

Almost as soon as the phenomenon was identified, some observers professed to see a seeming sheep-like strain in the behavior of U.S. enterprises: when one of them located a subsidiary in a foreign country, according to some observers, others had a strong tendency to follow. Soon familiar phrases were being used to describe the behavior, such as the bandwagon effect and the follow-the-leader syndrome.

Though behavioral patterns of this sort have been described in the literature for a good many years, the assumption that they existed has been based mainly on casual observation and anecdotal materials. The data bank of the Harvard Multinational Enterprise Project, which became available to scholars in 1969, afforded a solid basis for testing whether the assumptions were grounded in fact. Nonetheless, when Mr. Knickerbocker decided to devote his doctoral thesis to an exploration of these patterns, he drew uneasy reactions from all of his faculty advisers, including myself. As we saw it, this was a high-risk undertaking; in the end, it could lead to nothing. The failure to detect any follow-the-leader tendency could easily be laid to poor measurement technique. And if the tendency were detected by some statistical means, the evidence might conceivably be explained away by rival hypotheses.

Nevertheless, we buried our collective misgivings and we made available the statistical and intellectual resources of the Multinational Enterprise Project, such as they were, for Knickerbocker's effort. His gamble paid off, for ultimately his dissertation was awarded the Richard D. Irwin Prize. An underlying Ford Foundation grant, which has financed the Multinational Enterprise Project since its inception, therefore can be credited with having borne a bit more fruit.

This book is not the last word on follow-the-leader behavior, nor is it intended to be. But it does change the basis of discussion in this field from one of casual conjecture to serious analysis. As a result of Knickerbocker's work, the presumption that a follow-the-leader pattern exists is now a good deal stronger. Much more is known about its configuration, including the characteristics of the industries in which it makes its strongest appearance. At least as important is the fact that the causes of such a behavioral pattern are now somewhat better understood. The pattern is not necessarily due to an irrational herd instinct. If a business is oligopolistic in structure and if a situation is fraught with uncertainty, then follow-the-leader behavior may be a justifiable strategy based on solid rational grounds.

But the story is Knickerbocker's, not mine. So I shall leave it to him to tell it.

RAYMOND VERNON

Herbert F. Johnson Professor of International
Business Management

Soldiers Field
Boston, Massachusetts
September 1972

Acknowledgments

Each year the Division of Research of the Harvard Business School publishes the doctoral dissertation awarded the Richard D. Irwin Prize. In 1972 it was my good fortune to win the award. This would never have happened, however, had it not been for the help and encouragement of others.

Professors Raymond Vernon, Jesse W. Markham, and Louis T. Wells, Jr., the members of my dissertation committee, freely gave me their assistance when I sought it and their reassurance when I needed it. Beyond this, they fully carried out the other half of their role. They rooted out many a weak spot in my work and constantly pressed me for higher standards of analysis and exposition. Whatever merit this book has is in good measure the result of their probings and proddings.

I am especially grateful to Professor Vernon for his guidance. At one point I thought I had a finished piece of research. He agreed that it was an adequate start, but he urged me to rethink it and to rewrite it. I did, and I attribute the fact that the dissertation now appears in published form to his good advice.

Four other individuals also made important contributions to this book. Professor Robert B. Stobaugh explored, in a preliminary way, the relationship between oligopolistic reaction and foreign direct investment. I borrowed some of his ideas and parts of his methodology. James W. Vaupel unraveled for me the subtleties of the Multinational Enterprise Project data bank and guided me through more than one statistical thicket. Miss Helen Ford contended with many of the nasty last-minute typing chores. And Miss Ruth Norton of the Harvard Business School's Division of Research edited my material and shepherded it into finished form. I appreciate all their efforts.

Notwithstanding the generous assistance from all those listed above, Nancy, my wife, helped most of all.

As is customary and proper, I fully accept the responsibility for any shortcomings in this book.

FREDERICK T. KNICKERBOCKER

Soldiers Field
Boston, Massachusetts
September 1972

Table of Contents

List of Tables

Oligopolistic Reaction
and Multinational Enterprise

1

Introduction

I. Purpose

Anyone who examines the history of large United States enterprises during the 20th century is bound to be struck by the
proliferation of their interests outside the borders of the United
States. Many reasons are advanced to explain the extraordi-
nary expansion of their realm of business activity. Among the
reasons asserted, one is that United States firms have become
international and more international still because of a type of
conduct called oligopolistic reaction: an interactive kind of
corporate behavior by which rival firms in an industry composed of a few large firms counter one another's moves by
making similar moves themselves. Testing the validity of this
assertion is the purpose of this book.

In order that the scope of analysis be within manageable
limits, inquiry will be restricted to investigating to what extent
and why in the post-World War II years U.S. companies
matched each other's *foreign direct investments*. Furthermore, inquiry will be confined to the domestic and foreign operations
of enterprises in *manufacturing industries only.*

To facilitate explaining what this study is about, it is useful
to disclose at the outset two findings that will be discussed in
Chapter 2. First, there is evidence that the member firms in a
number of United States industries have tended to bunch together their direct investments in foreign countries. Second,
from data developed in this study and from the work of others,
there is evidence that U.S. enterprises in the forefront of inter-

national expansion typically have inhabited oligopolistically structured industries. Standing alone, however, these two pieces of evidence do not demonstrate that the bunching together of foreign investments has been in any way related to the desire of oligopolists to checkmate the moves of rivals. The remaining chapters are devoted in part to making the case for such a relationship.

As one might guess, if for no other reason than that it would be surprising to find absolutely uniform behavior among firms operating under different industrial conditions, the evidence shows that the tendency of rival firms to bunch their investments abroad together has varied from one industry to the next. This variation in how firms interacted with one another is related to certain industry and firm characteristics and to the strategies firms adopted to enlarge their stakes abroad. The chapters that follow are also devoted to making that case.

Market characteristics, too, have affected the conduct of United States enterprises. Chapter 8 presents the evidence on this point and discusses the reasons why United States firms have tended to bunch their direct investments together in some countries and not in others.

Since all the evidence to be examined relates to foreign direct investment, definition of this form of investment is required from the start. When an enterprise invests in assets outside its home country in order to control, partially or fully, the operation of these assets, the resulting capital flow is called a foreign direct investment.[1] Any overseas subsidiary that manu-

---

[1] The U.S. Department of Commerce defines direct investment abroad as: ". . . the flow of U.S. capital into foreign business enterprise in which U.S. residents have significant control. Hence, the capital movements are deemed to be foreign extensions of the management interests of the parent corporation. The distinction between long-term investments in equity securities and direct investment is made on the basis of ownership. Investment is considered direct when the U.S. individual or company owns more than 10 percent of the foreign concern." U.S. Department of Commerce, *Dictionary of Economic and Statistical Terms* (Washington: Government Printing Office, 1969).

For a discussion of what determines the ownership pattern of foreign subsidiaries, the reader is referred to Lawrence Franko, "Strategy Choice and Multinational Cor-

factures and sells products constitutes a foreign direct investment. But whereas the first subsidiary established in a given industry, in a given country, will be regarded as an aggressive investment, all others established in the same industry, in the same country, to manufacture and sell products in competition with those of the first subsidiary will be regarded as defensive investments.

With the difference between aggressive and defensive foreign direct investment distinguished, the purpose of this inquiry can be stated more precisely. The study is concerned with defensive investment and is directed at answering the following questions. Were the forces that induced aggressive and defensive foreign direct investments the same, or were firms that made defensive investments influenced by some forces in addition to those that prompted the first firm to move; were they reacting to the moves of recognized rivals? Why have firms been more inclined to make defensive investments in some industries than in others, in some countries than in others?

Before the search for answers can begin, however, the first order of business is to spell out the *a priori* reasons for believing that large U.S. enterprises have a predilection for countering the moves of rivals and for believing that this predilection has influenced their foreign investment decisions. This task requires consideration of notions taken from the theory of oligopoly. In the next section of this chapter concepts and terms relating to oligopoly are defined and used to sketch out firm behavior under oligopoly conditions. The discussion is both rudimentary and abstract; its purpose is simply to convey some notion of what the terms mean as they are used in the coming chapters. In the subsequent section, however, these abstractions are linked to a model of U.S. industry's international expansion to create the conceptual framework for this study.

---

porate Tolerance for Joint Ventures with Foreign Partners" (unpublished doctoral dissertation, Harvard Business School, 1969). The issue will also be discussed in several forthcoming studies by Professor Louis T. Wells of the Harvard Business School.

II. Oligopoly Concepts and Terminology

Oligopoly defined.—The term oligopoly defines the type of market structure that exists when there are only a few sellers, when these few sell products that are close substitutes for one another, and when, as a third condition, there is substantial market interdependence among the competitive policies of these firms.

Professor Caves's description of oligopoly underscores the importance of seller interdependence:

> The essence of oligopoly is that firms are few enough to recognize the impact of their actions on their rivals and thus on the market as a whole. . . . When an industry contains one firm (monopoly) or many firms (pure competition), the individual sellers react only to impersonal market forces. In oligopoly they react to one another in a direct and personal fashion. This inevitable interaction of sellers in an oligopolistic market we call mutual interdependence.
>
> Where mutual interdependence exists, sellers do not just take into account the effects of their actions on the total market . . . , they also take into account the effects of their actions on one another. Oligopoly becomes something like a poker game.[2]

Note that oligopoly is a definition of both the *structure* of a market and of the *behavior* of the firms selling in the market.

Even though oligopoly refers, in the strictest sense, to a market situation, the term is frequently applied to any industry made up of a few firms serving a market. Professor Bain uses the term in this way when he defines oligopolistic industries as those

> . . . in which seller concentration is high. Strictly, these are industries in which the number of sellers is small and in which

---

[2] Richard E. Caves, *American Industry: Structure, Conduct, Performance* (2d ed.; Englewood Cliffs: Prentice-Hall, 1967).

every seller supplies a large enough proportion of industry output that his own changes in output or price will perceptibly
affect the prices or sales volumes of the other firms in the industry.[3]

In the coming chapters, the term oligopoly will be used most
frequently in the industry sense.

Oligopolistic reaction.—Whereas the theory of pure competition requires no assumption that the acts of one firm will induce responses from fellow industry members, the theory of oligopoly rests upon just such an assumption. This premise that
firms are mutually interdependent means that the behavior of
firms in oligopolies will tend toward a pattern of action-reac-
tion, move-countermove. Each oligopolist, as if he were
playing a game of chess, combines moves to improve his own
offensive position with moves to offset his opponent's attempts
to build an attack. Oligopolistic reaction is the term that will
be used throughout the study to describe this move-countermove type of firm behavior. This term, rather than defensive
investment, will be used most frequently because it emphasizes
that the interplay among firms takes place within a specific
type of industry structure.

A highly simplified example illustrates why oligopolists tend
to behave in such a fashion. Picture a market situation composed of a few sellers. Each seller recognizes that it has open to
it a large number of competitive policies and strategies that
could result in its gaining a competitive advantage over its rivals.[4] Now suppose one of the rivals adopts one of these courses

---

[3] Joe S. Bain, *Industrial Organization* (2d ed.; New York: John Wiley and Sons, 1968),
p. 114.

[4] As Jesse W. Markham points out: "The modern business firm may typically confront relatively few rivals, but it has available a wide variety of business policies and
strategies to employ against them. Advertising and research budgets, product change,
marketing methods, and non-price terms of trade, as well as prices, are variables over
which most oligopolists exercise some degree of discretion, and how they exercise it is
the essence of the oligopoly problem." Jesse W. Markham, "Oligopoly," in David L.
Sills (ed.), *International Encyclopedia of the Social Sciences*, XI (1968), p. 286.

of action and the others do nothing out of the ordinary. If the advantage is substantial enough and if market demand is relatively static, the firm with the advantage can increase its market share (remember the products are substitutable) at the expense of the rivals; one firm's gain is the rivals' loss. Or if the advantage is substantial enough but market demand is increasing, the firm with the advantage can capture a disproportionately high share of demand growth; one firm grows rapidly, the others less so.

If, as is the common case, sales growth is accompanied by an increment in physical, financial, or human assets, the firm upping its share of market or of market growth stands a good chance of increasing its competitive capabilities relative to those of its rivals. And so long as its growth is not accompanied by diseconomies, the firm in the front rank may extend its competitive lead.

Of course the rivals of the firm that initially gained the competitive edge recognize that, unless they do something, they may face a prospect like that described above. Accordingly, they try to nullify the anticipated consequence of their rivals' moves by countering with similar moves or with some kind of blocking strategy. In a general way countering accomplishes one of two things. Either the countering firms acquire about the same advantages as the firm that made the initial move, so that a new competitive balance is established in the industry, or the countering firms force the firm with the advantage to forego exploiting it by the threat of intensifying competition in the industry to the point where all rivals suffer. In this case the old competitive balance is restored.

Oligopolistic equilibrium.—So long as aggressive moves provoke defensive moves, rivalry among oligopolists can potentially deteriorate into mutually destructive competition. The classic example of this is price warfare. Each firm underprices its rivals to the point where no firm in the industry can earn a profit. Oligopolists are well aware that such rivalry is a game where nobody wins.

Over time, therefore, oligopolists may reach an understanding (explicit or implicit) to avoid excessively intense rivalry. Instead, they introduce order in the market. Each firm restrains its own aggressive behavior with the expectation that rivals will exercise the same restraint. Together they shy away from conduct, e.g., price competition, that has direct, unfavorable economic consequences. Rather they emphasize modes of competition, like advertising, that may expand demand, or at least sustain it, for the benefit of all the members of the industry. And they seek to maintain the stability of the situation by mimicking each other's moves. With all rivals having roughly the same competitive capabilities, there is little reason for any one rival to expect that it can, with impunity, improve its market position at the expense of others. When this state of affairs exists among sellers, their industry is said to be in oligopolistic equilibrium.

Still this new order of things is a tenuous one in a dynamic situation. A few industries, especially those characterized by gradual change, may perpetuate this state of disciplined rivalry from one market to the next. But in industries where such factors as new technology or new buyer preferences produce rapid change, oligopolists may resort to quite aggressive rivalry to seize opportunities. They may believe that the chance of gaining even a short-lived advantage over rivals is worth the risks involved, and hence the equilibrium may be periodically disrupted until the others move in to restore the balance.

But what do the abstract notions reviewed above have to do with foreign direct investment? Establishing that connection calls for the development of a chain of ideas that begins with discussion of the fundamental forces that prompted U.S. firms to look outside the United States for business opportunities.

III. A Conceptual Scheme

Oligopolistic reaction: a partial explanation for foreign direct investment.—Although this study focuses on the effects that oligopolistic reaction has had on the course of U.S. foreign direct investment, it will not be argued that this one type of firm behavior is the sole or even principal explanation for why U.S. firms have invested overseas. To the contrary, it is important to establish the limits of the explanatory power of oligopolistic reaction and to show how oligopolistic reaction fits into a general model that seems to explain much about the internationalization of U.S. business.

Oligopolistic reaction must be considered within a broad conceptual framework for two reasons. First, it is a description of essentially defensive firm behavior. That is, if firm A makes a move, say investing abroad, then the concept of oligopolistic reaction tells us something about what firm B, a rival of A, is likely to do. But the concept of oligopolistic reaction does not explain why firm A moved in the first place. Some notions about the fundamental forces that have sparked foreign direct investment are needed to explain A's behavior. Once these fundamental forces are set forth, it will then be possible to relate the role of oligopolistic reaction to the multinational spread of U.S. business.

Second, the concept of oligopolistic reaction cannot explain, in and of itself, why it is that some U.S. industries have been heavily engaged in direct investment abroad while others have not. There is ample evidence, which will be examined presently, that U.S. direct investment abroad has been dominated by firms that have operated under oligopoly conditions at home and abroad. Although the concept of oligopolistic reaction does help to make it clear why the firms in oligopolistically structured industries have moved abroad almost *en masse,* the concept does not explain why it is that these industries, and not others, have been in the forefront of the international expansion of U.S. business. Put another way, the notion of oligopolistic reaction helps to make comprehensible the proliferation of U.S.-controlled foreign subsidiaries once one or two firms in certain U.S. industries have led the way overseas, but an understanding of the factors that have determined which industries have moved abroad calls for broader and more powerful concepts.

From general to specific concepts in three steps.—Analysis of the ideas basic to this study starts then with the proposition advanced in the preceding section that oligopolistic reaction describes firm behavior induced by a subset of forces within a more general set of forces that have motivated foreign direct investment. The three sets of questions listed below, which define the topics to be discussed in the remainder of this chapter, illustrate how the analysis will narrow down from consideration of a general theory of the conditions and forces leading to the international expansion of U.S. business to consideration of some specific propositions of why it is that rivals in oligopolistically structured industries have been inclined to match the foreign direct investments of each other:

1. Why is it that some, though not all, U.S. manufacturing industries have extended their activities beyond the borders of the United States? What has made it possible for the member firms in these industries to do so? Over the years, what has been the sequence of steps taken by manufacturing enterprises to extend their activities into foreign markets?

2. Why is it that the bulk of international expansion of U.S. business has taken place in industries that have been oligopolistically structured?

3. Why, under oligopoly conditions, have rival firms tended to match the foreign direct investments of each other? What were the risks oligopolists faced if they did not counter the moves of industry rivals?

Once responses to these questions have been provided and once the links between the three sets of questions have been established, examination of the research evidence will indicate the extent to which the behavior of U.S. enterprises has been consistent with the way that large firms, operating under oligopoly conditions, could be expected to behave as they responded to the basic inducements prompting them to expand overseas. But first, what were these fundamental inducements?

The product cycle model.—The set of forces that have prompted U.S. manufacturing enterprises to expand their business activities beyond the borders of the United States are understandable in terms of a product cycle model. Like any model of a nonphysical process, this one cannot account for all the particularities in a chain of events as complex and variegated as the international proliferation of U.S. industry. Nevertheless the model explains much about how and why this proliferation took place, and, perhaps of greater importance, it stands the challenge of empirical testing.

It is now well established that the experience of many products in the market place can be characterized in life cycle terms: birth, rapid growth, maturity, and senescence. For reasons to be spelled out, U.S. manufacturing industry traditionally has concentrated much of its effort on the first two phases of this cycle, that is, on product discovery and market introduction, and on market saturation. In those U.S. industries where, for one after another generation of products, attention centered on the early phases of products' lives, the member firms acquired certain special capabilities that subsequently become the cornerstones upon which the firms built their multinational operations.

The product cycle model links the factors that have accounted for U.S. industry's emphasis on the discovery and market introduction of new products to the factors that have invested U.S. firms with both the capability and the desire to penetrate foreign markets. In so doing, the model ties longstanding and fundamental characteristics of the U.S. economy to the international spread of U.S. business.

Since both the model and the evidence in support of the model have been elaborated comprehensively by Professor Raymond Vernon, only a bare-bones description of the model follows.[5] For the purposes of this study the utility of the model

---

[5] For a quite thorough description of the model and of the evidence supporting the

INTRODUCTION   11

goes beyond the fact that it identifies the capabilities U.S. firms have acquired which enabled them to expand abroad. These capabilities have had a second role: they have been critical determinants of the structure of the industries involved in international expansion. That is, manufacturing enterprises able to expand abroad have had their abilities to do so nurtured under oligopolistic conditions at home. According to the model, how has all this come about?

From about the 1850s onward several unique and persistent characteristics of the U.S. economy, labor scarcity and resource abundance on the supply side and rapidly rising per capita incomes on the demand side, led many U.S. manufacturers to concentrate on developing products that were labor-saving or that satisfied high-income consumers. Each generation of products would meet the needs of the U.S. economy for a while. Yet economic growth fostered the need for newer and better versions of labor-saving and high-income goods. To respond to the changes in demand manufacturers had to make product innovation an essential and continuous corporate activity. Over time R&D became inbred in successful firms. But beyond this, the breadth of the U.S. economy in geographical terms and the depth of the economy in income distribution terms compelled these product-innovating firms to master the mass production and mass distribution of their goods.

Why was it though that the production of labor-saving and high-income goods started in the United States? Why did not well-established European firms become the initial suppliers of these goods? After all, in the second half of the 1800s and the early years of the 1900s many U.S. manufacturers were fledglings compared with European producers. What considerations dictated supplying the U.S. market for these particular types of goods from plants located in the United States rather than from plants sited abroad?

Locational advantages are the most obvious. U.S. producers

---

model, see Raymond Vernon, *Sovereignty at Bay: The Multinational Spread of U.S. Enterprises* (New York: Basic Books, 1971).

had lower transportation costs than foreign producers. And in the case of at least some goods U.S. producers did not have to surmount the barriers to trade that faced foreign producers. But apart from conventional locational advantages, U.S. producers had a leg up over foreign manufacturers because the U.S. firms were close to the market place.

To be sure, proximity to the market place probably always confers some selling advantage, but because the emphasis of so much of U.S. manufacturing activity was on product innovation and product upgrading, market proximity was especially important. This was so because market reception of new products was usually uncertain. The final form products took was seldom fixed when products were first put on the market. Manufacturers needed rapid feedback from the market in order to modify their products or alternatively to modify the ways they marketed their products. Production in the United States assured a rapidity and clarity of communication between the market place and the manufacturer not available to the firm located abroad.

Beyond the uncertainty surrounding acceptable product characteristics, the size of the total market for newly developed products was frequently uncertain as well. Here again, producers in the United States were in a better position than those located abroad to receive timely and accurate information on the growth of demand and, as a consequence, to adjust productive capacity to variation in demand.

Then, too, U.S. industry's emphasis on developing and introducing products with high innovative content tended to protect U.S. manufacturers from import competition because of the inherent low price elasticity of the products. In the early stages of their life cycles products are usually technologically differentiated, or easily subject to differentiation by marketing efforts, with the result that for the many U.S. firms that concentrated on bringing new products to the market low production costs were seldom prerequisite for commercial success. It follows that foreign manufacturers, even those with production costs below the costs of U.S. manufacturers, had little advantage over U.S. firms since the characteristics of U.S. demand for products with high innovative content made price a secondary matter.

Highly differentiated products affected the location of production sites in yet another way. Since U.S. manufacturers not uncommonly earned monopoly or quasi-monopoly profits—the result of either product uniqueness or product differentiation—they had little goad to search outside the United States for lower cost production sites. The upshot of this and all the other foregoing points is that the bulk of U.S. demand for labor-saving or high-income goods was supplied by manufacturing enterprises located at home.

To recapitulate, the industrial history of the United States shows that the member firms in a number of U.S. manufacturing industries devoted much of their attention and energy to the development, mass production, and mass marketing of goods uniquely suited to the U.S. market. A convenient shorthand term describes the activities of these firms: they engaged in "product pioneering." In the industries characterized by product pioneering, supply from abroad was seldom a significant factor. As a consequence, throughout the latter half of the 1800s and the first few decades of the 1900s the member firms in these industries acquired a bundle of capabilities that were almost impossible for foreign manufacturers to acquire since they, the foreign firms, had no cause and little opportunity to adapt to the U.S. economic environment.

This bundle of special capabilities subsequently became the foundation upon which the international expansion of U.S. manufacturing industry was based. This fact has much to do with the evidence presented throughout this entire study. The data will relate to the overseas activities of U.S. manufacturers within a dozen broadly defined industrial categories. One or more of three characteristics typically mark all the firms in the twelve industries: (1) the firms conduct extensive research and development, or (2) they employ complex, high-technology productive methods, or (3) they engage in vigorous and sophisticated marketing activities. Why these characteristics and not others?

The special capabilities of the product-pioneering firms.—Over the years those U.S. manufacturers that concentrated on product innovation acquired sophisticated research and development skills. Of perhaps even greater importance, these manufacturers developed the organizational skills to manage large R&D activities and to integrate these activities with other important enterprise functions. In addition, product pioneers learned to bridge the gap between the laboratory and the market place. The results were organizational designs and practices making U.S. industrial R&D especially responsive to market needs. And as a natural spill-off from their R&D efforts, U.S. manufacturers inherited a mounting number of patentable products or processes. When the product-pioneering firms eventually marched abroad, foreign firms were seldom in a position to compete, lacking as they generally did anything comparable to the U.S. firms' R&D skills and their backlog of legally protected innovations.

The product-pioneering U.S. firms acquired other technological capabilities as well. Many learned how to mass-manufacture complex, high-quality products. Henry Ford's assembly line epitomizes this capability. In contrast, foreign manufacturers had little occasion to internalize mass production skills since they frequently supplied only small or nascent national markets.

Then, too, the large size of the U.S. market often necessitated mass distribution and mass selling. The product pioneers confronted the problems of mass marketing and evolved solutions to the problems long before manufacturers abroad came to grips with the same challenges. As in the case of spill-off from R&D, the U.S. firms that emphasized marketing harvested a mounting number of trademarks and brand names that, in time, would become the basis of consumer franchises around the world.

Along with acquiring specific research, production, and marketing skills, the product pioneers mastered the knack of coordinating all the business functions involved in bringing a continual stream of new products to the market. It was not, therefore, by accident that the United States was regarded for many years as the source of the most advanced knowledge of administrative art and science. Thus, general managerial skills buttressed all the other special capabilities of the product pioneers.

To sum up, those U.S. manufacturing enterprises that focused their energies on products in the early stages of their life cycles acquired technological and organizational capabilities that could be replicated by foreign manufacturers only with difficulty and only years after the capabilities became commonplace among large U.S. manufacturers.

The expansion of the product pioneers into world markets.— After a lag of some years the supply and demand characteristics of developed countries outside the United States, particularly countries in Western Europe, began to parallel those in the United States. Consequently, products designed to satisfy these characteristics in the United States proved aptly suited for foreign markets. The initial response to this opportunity by U.S. manufacturing enterprises was exporting. The shipment overseas of products with high technological content or of products that represented the latest and most sophisticated version of goods within a product class became the backbone of U.S. export trade in manufactured goods.

In time, however, matured products exported from the United States, those no longer in the early stages of their product cycles, tended to become standardized. The technology for their production became stabilized and lost its esoteric quality. As the knowledge of how to produce the goods became generally available, manufacture by foreign firms became possible. At the same time, product features once considered unique by foreign buyers of the U.S. exports came to be regarded as common. As a consequence, demand for these maturing products became more price-elastic. When for the first time production costs became determinants of product success, low-cost foreign manufacturers finally gained a competitive edge over U.S. producers. As the advantages that U.S. firms had in producing these export items declined, foreign rivals began to manufacture the products to meet local demand.

With their exports in jeopardy, U.S. product-pioneering manufacturers faced several alternatives to preserve their position in foreign markets.

1. They could abandon the export of older products in anticipation that the next generation of products would furnish them with a new, viable export base.

2. They could rent to foreign producers, by way of licensing agreements, that part of their technical expertise not yet widely disseminated. In the case of this second alternative U.S. manufacturers could earn some return on their knowledge even if they could no longer exploit the knowledge through exports.

3. The product-pioneering U.S. firms could take the plunge and invest in overseas manufacturing plants from which they could supply their threatened markets. By switching from exporting to production abroad U.S. manufacturers could match any production advantages that local producers might have, thereby negating the threat of price competition. Direct investment therefore made it possible for the product pioneers to perpetuate their overseas revenue streams from the products they had developed at some time in the past in the United States.

Most of the product pioneers chose a mixed bag of all three alternatives. Yet, as foreign demand grew and as U.S. businessmen learned how to cope with manufacturing and selling abroad, foreign direct investment became the preferred route by which U.S. enterprises prolonged returns from abroad on older capabilities or exploited newer capabilities abroad. Direct investment became preferred because the product pioneers came to recognize that it afforded them a better opportunity to manage the overseas exploitation of their special capabilities than did any other approach to penetrating foreign markets.

Of course, local companies had certain distinct advantages over incoming U.S. firms. The cost of information to U.S. investors was certainly higher than to firms operating in home environments. Similarly, the costs of communication and organization—the costs of linking foreign subsidiaries with U.S. headquarters—were higher for U.S. firms than for firms operating in their home markets. And local firms could expect to receive somewhat better treatment from their governments than would foreign-based investors.

Nevertheless, the product pioneers' organizational and technological capabilities counterbalanced the advantages held by local manufacturers. For example, by combining their special manufacturing skills with the factor inputs available in foreign countries, U.S. manufacturing subsidiaries matched or even bettered the production costs of local competitors. Likewise in marketing, U.S. subsidiaries, by drawing on the reservoir of marketing skills in the parent company, could match or better the selling efforts of local competitors. Also, in the case of general managerial effectiveness, U.S. subsidiaries probably had some edge over local competitors as a result of organizational skills acquired in the United States and transferred overseas. In a few words, U.S. product pioneers stormed foreign markets with competitive weapons forged at home.

A cautionary note is in order here. The set of notions just advanced, direct investment overseas by U.S. enterprises in response to the erosion of locational and informational advantages that had initially dictated exporting products from the United States, represents a powerful model of the motivations prompting U.S. business to expand abroad and of the process by which this came to pass. The model depicts fundamental forces at work. Yet a number of other factors and events certainly triggered U.S. firms to respond to these fundamental forces.

From time to time obstacles to trade, e.g., tariff and nontariff barriers, threatened the product pioneer's export markets. Direct investment abroad circumvented many such obstacles. Or, in the case of products whose commercial success depended upon close contact between the producer and the consumer, e.g., after-sales servicing, U.S. firms opted to invest abroad for marketing reasons. With other products, the need for their adaptation to local technical requirements or to local consumer tastes argued for production on the scene. In yet other instances when an important industrial customer of a U.S. firm established a subsidiary abroad, the U.S. supplier may have felt obliged to establish its own subsidiary to protect the supplier-customer relationship.

Other circumstances, usually associated with only specific types of foreign countries, also sparked direct investment. For example, less developed countries often barred the importation of certain classes of goods in order to stimulate local production. U.S. firms either made direct investments or saw their stakes in the less developed countries disappear.

Although the list can go on and on, the critical point to note is that regardless of the circumstances that provoked any particular foreign direct investment, the product cycle model suggests that the fundamental consideration underlying such undertakings has been the desire of U.S. businessmen to exploit overseas the novel skills that their firms acquired in the course of satisfying U.S. demand.

The link between the product cycle model and oligopolistic market structures.—The fundamental conditions that prompted U.S. product-pioneering firms to expand abroad also tended to concentrate the U.S. industries populated by these firms. Almost all of the factors that are usually regarded as leading to oligopolistic industry structures prevailed among the product pioneers.

For example, such firms operated in technologically uncertain environments. In the second half of the 1800s and in the early years of the 1900s the failure rate among innovating firms was high. As a consequence, in U.S. manufacturing industry potential rivals were frequently weeded out. The demise of many small automobile manufacturers and of many small farm equipment manufacturers in the first several decades of the 1900s are familiar examples of firm attrition in technologically unstable industries that led, eventually, to concentrated industry structures.

Scale economies also tended to limit to a few the number of firms that could compete successfully in any one industry. Recall that the firms under consideration have been not only product innovators but also mass producers and mass merchandisers. Once only a few of these firms attained any appreciable size in an industry, scale economies gave them an almost insurmountable competitive edge over other industry entrants. The history of the Singer Company, a prototype of the product-pioneering firm, illustrates this point. Singer's early success rested on its fine, though not absolutely unique, sewing machine. Yet the remarkable growth of the company depended as much on its ability to mass-manufacture quality machines at a reasonable cost and to mass-market and service its machines as on the machines' special features. Its innovational lead, coupled with production and marketing scale economies, permitted Singer to dominate its market for over half a century.

Other scale economies, such as those available in R&D and in organization, fortified the competitive strength of product-pioneering firms. Companies like General Electric, National Cash Register, and International Harvester were in the vanguard of U.S. investors overseas, and although their product development efforts in the decades around the turn of the century seem rudimentary by current standards, their ability to exploit a steady stream of in-house generated innovations gave them a competitive advantage over domestic and foreign rivals.

Regardless of which scale economy it was of special importance to each product-pioneering firm, the advantages of scale were clear. And because large-scale economies and large firm size were usually two sides of the same coin, the product pioneers were in the forefront of the merger movements that swept the United States in the late 1800s and in the post-World War I years.

Barriers to entry also reinforced the trend toward industrial concentration. The loci of patents, trademarks, brand names, and differentiated products were to be found among the product-pioneering firms. Moreover, because these firms concentrated on the development and manufacture of products with high technological content, they were usually capital-intensive and skill-intensive. Entry into the industries dominated by the product pioneers often called for large, lumpy investments and more than average inputs of organizational skills. As a consequence, seller concentration in such industries, once established, seldom tended to break down.

The preceding few points add up to no more than a cursory review of forces leading to oligopolistic industry structures. Bear in mind, however, that the aim here is not to detail the causes of industrial concentration in the United States. Rather the aim is to establish that the economic factors that tended to bring about concentration of the manufacturing industries in which the product-innovating companies made their homes were the same factors that accounted for these firms becoming the United States' most active exporters and foreign direct investors. The nub of the case being made here is that the special technological and organizational capabilities acquired by these firms first invested them with market power at home and, at a later date, invested them with market power abroad. Accordingly, oligopoly conditions have constituted the normal world-wide milieu of U.S. product-pioneering firms.

In relation to the special capabilities of the product-pioneering firms, two final points need to be made before we can consider why these firms tended to interact with one another in the course of expanding their interests abroad. The first point concerns the marginal cost of exploiting the product pioneers' special skills in foreign markets. Once they absorbed the costs of acquiring their core capabilities, costs became sunk. True, from time to time product pioneers had to invest in upgrading their skills and even in developing new ones. Still, their costs of doing so were probably lower than those associated with the initial acquisition of their skills.

Now, if the product pioneers could exploit their core capabilities in one foreign market after another, and by dint of organizational learning decrease their marginal costs while doing so, their returns on the capabilities could increase markedly. Thus the profit potential inherent in their special capabilities was great once the product pioneers could begin to bring down the cost of successive market exploitation of the capabilities.

Second, more than likely the product pioneers tried to optimize corporate-wide returns from their core capabilities rather than to optimize the returns from each individual foreign operation. Certainly most product-pioneering firms were sophisticated enough to recognize that the reverse strategy, i.e., optimization of the returns from individual operations, could lead to suboptimization for the total corporate system. To be sure, in their early years of international activity, some of the product pioneers may have lacked the organizational skills to make system-wide optimization possible or the appropriate mixture of foreign and domestic operations to make system-wide optimization feasible. Nonetheless, product pioneers must have recognized the increasing importance of system-wide benefits associated with each new foreign venture.

To the extent that product pioneers were prompted to enlarge their overseas commitments by the prospects of high, system-wide, marginal returns on their core skills, an important corollary follows. Whenever one or more rivals of a product-pioneering firm (call it firm A) took steps in regard to a foreign market (call it country X) that could be perceived by the management of A as weakening the firm's ability to compete in country X, A's management would believe that the firm faced important risks. For A the risks could be at three different levels of severity.

On the first level, the rivals' moves could imperil the income A was earning in country X. On the second level, if A's operations in country X were an essential link in its corporate network, e.g., its logistics network, the competitors' moves could imperil A's corporate-wide earnings on the product or product line under threat. Finally, on the third level, the moves by the rivals could result in their acquiring capabilities beyond those they already had. In this last case the entire competitive equilibrium within the industry could be disrupted, and A might find itself (both at home and abroad) at a competitive disadvantage with regard to many or all of its products.

Presently we shall examine these risks in detail. First, however, it is necessary to consider the role of uncertainty in the process of foreign expansion, for it appears that the strategy the product pioneers commonly adopted to cope with competitive risk was dictated by the high level of uncertainty inherent in doing business across national boundaries.

The propositions about uncertainty and risk that follow are crucial ones. They are advanced as the core explanation for oligopolistic behavior among the product-pioneering firms. Bear in mind that up to this point we have been examining a set of concepts that explain why all product-pioneering firms could, and would want to, enlarge their stakes in foreign markets. From this point on, however, we shall be considering how interaction among industry rivals added momentum to the overseas proliferation of U.S.-controlled interests.

Uncertainty avoidance and risk minimization: determinants of firm conduct.

—Decision makers in product-pioneering firms commonly faced a highly uncertain environment when they set up their outposts around the globe. Since they committed resources under conditions of partial ignorance, the outcomes from these commitments were hard to predict. Successes could follow, but so too could disasters.

In the literature on organizational behavior there is sufficient evidence to make it clear that businessmen are strongly motivated to do whatever they can to avoid uncertainty since the more there is of it, the less possible becomes purposeful management. Cyert and March, for example, conclude that firms strive to avoid uncertainty by trying to create negotiated and controllable environments.[6] Though much of the literature on organizational behavior is based on studying the conduct of firms within their home country, it does not seem unreasonable to expect that firms strive to avoid uncertainty as much in their international operations as in their domestic operations, especially if the world abroad is perceived as even more uncertain than the world at home.

That uncertainty abounded for the product-pioneering firms is clear. When they contemplated their initial penetrations of foreign markets, they typically possessed only fragmentary information on a whole set of relevant foreign market variables, e.g., the characteristics of supply and demand, the nature of local competition, the requirements for and availability of local financing, the mores of doing business, the dimensions and applicability of local laws, and the import of governmental policies. Furthermore, any one or all of these variables could change, but novice U.S. firms had, at best, imperfect information networks to monitor for change. Of course, over time, the product innovators could, and did, upgrade their information-gathering skills. Nonetheless, each new market represented something of *terra incognita.*

On top of this, the technological uncertainty that inhered in the product-pioneering industries was probably perceived as increasing when the industries' members expanded abroad since they were introducing their products into new untested markets.

To compound the problem of uncertainty, the costs and organizational effort involved in acquiring the necessary information about foreign markets could frequently exceed those involved in acquiring information in the United States. In short, for the product pioneers moving abroad, uncertainties were many and the costs of resolving them were high.

Still, uncertainty could be reduced to some extent. The se-

---

[6] Richard M. Cyert and James G. March, *A Behavioral Theory of the Firm* (Englewood Cliffs: Prentice-Hall, 1963), pp. 119–120.

quence in which the product pioneers commonly deepened their involvement in foreign markets, i.e., exporting, licensing, direct investment, aided them in overcoming, in stages, their informational shortcomings. Each stage of foreign involvement contributed to organizational learning and laid a stepping-stone for the next stage of involvement. Two important consequences followed from this incremental approach. The product pioneers broadened their abilities to scan the world for opportunities, and they lowered their marginal costs of reducing the uncertainty associated with each new foreign venture. Although these consequences reinforced the product pioneers' desires to expand abroad, they also affected the competitive hazards in the game.

When only one firm in an industry upgraded its scanning and information-gathering skills, it buttressed its competitive capacity. But when all the principal rivals in an industry upgraded these skills, the new capabilities became a mixed blessing, for then each rival could identify and respond to new overseas opportunities or threats more decisively than in the past. Ironically, therefore, as the member firms in the product-pioneering industries were gaining experience in world-wide operations, they were trading off uncertainty for risk because competitors were becoming increasingly ready and capable to commit resources all over the world.

Under the circumstances, prudence argued for the adoption of the risk-minimizing strategy of industry rivals matching each other's moves.[7] To illustrate, if firm B matched, move for move, the acts of its rival, firm A, B would have roughly the same chance as A to exploit each new foreign market opportunity. Thus for each new market penetrated by both A and B, B's gains, either in terms of earnings or in terms of the acquisition of new capabilities, would parallel those of A. And if some of firm A's moves turned out to be failures, B's losses would be

---

[7] The notion of risk-minimization advanced here is adapted from Raymond Vernon, *Manager in the International Economy* (Englewood Cliffs: Prentice-Hall, 1968), Chapter 10.

in the range of those of A. Neither firm would be better or worse off. From the point of view of firm B, this matching strategy guaranteed that its competitive capabilities would remain roughly in balance with those of firm A.

Some observers of international business describe this risk-minimizing strategy in game theory terms. Aharoni, for one, believes that a "bandwagon effect" is a leading force prompting U.S. firms to undertake direct overseas investments:

> . . . when several companies in the same industry went abroad, others felt compelled to follow suit in order to maintain their relative size and their relative rate of growth.[8]

Aharoni contends that such behavior is a manifestation of enterprise minimax strategy: of a firm "imitating the commitments of a leader on the grounds that one is less vulnerable if his exposures are the same as those of his principal competitors." [9]

Regardless of how one thinks about risk-minimization in theoretical terms, it is clear that businessmen recognize the countering motivation. In reviewing his industry survey, Robinson reported that when managements of 205 firms were asked to list the major factors that led to their investing abroad, the answer in 37% of the cases was "the desire to match or forestall a competitive move." [10]

For businessmen, countering was a form of insurance. The premium firms paid to insure the perpetuation of competitive balance was the cost involved in making a matching move. One reason firms were prepared to pay the premium was that its cost tended to go down since the marginal costs of each additional step into the international market place tended to go

---

[8] Yair Aharoni, *The Foreign Investment Decision Process* (Boston: Division of Research, Harvard Business School, 1966), pp. 65–66.

[9] *Ibid.,* p. 66.

[10] Harry J. Robinson, *The Motivation and Flow of Private Foreign Investment* (Menlo Park: Stanford Research Institute, 1961), p. 24.

down. But the fundamental reason for paying the premium was that its costs were at least partially predictable whereas the costs to a firm, if it did not counter the moves of a rival, were often unpredictable and could, very possibly, far exceed those of countering.

A few specific examples will make clear the risks a firm could face if it did not adopt the policy of matching competitors' moves. The following examples are based on a two-firm industry, but it is obvious that the duopoly model could be extended to the general case of oligopoly.

Picture the situation where firms A and B, two product-pioneering manufacturers, export competing products to foreign country X. Now, suppose A established a manufacturing subsidiary in X. B, uncertain of the production economies, if any, that A might gain by manufacturing locally, faces the possibility that it could be underpriced by A in the market place. By establishing its own manufacturing subsidiary, B can match the production costs of A and thereby preserve its market share should A resort to price competition.

In reality the dilemma facing firm B is usually much more complex than that pictured above. When firm A starts to manufacture in country X, its subsidiary management, and perhaps its headquarters management, are exposed to factor inputs and technologies that may differ in terms of type, quality, or cost from those previously encountered in the United States or elsewhere. In responding to this new matrix of factors, firm A may find that it can use new raw materials, or it may devise new manufacturing processes, or it may even uncover new product possibilities. Moreover, information about the discoveries can be transferred to other parts of A's organization. Armed with whatever new capability it has acquired in country X, firm A may be able to out-compete B in country X, in other foreign markets, and, perhaps, even in the United States. If B decides not to match A's move, B may be unwittingly jeopardizing its world-wide competitive position.

It is not hard for the management of firm B to picture other risks in A's move. Once A manufactures within country X, it may be able to convince the local government to put up tariff or nontariff barriers to the importation of B's products. Or A may be able to prevent B from investing in country X by convincing the local government that the market can absorb only the output from one efficiently sized plant.

Of course, B can only speculate on the risks it may run by not matching A. But that is the whole point. Until B parallels A's move, B has little way of knowing what threats are real and what threats are imaginary. Matching A both removes this uncertainty for B and preserves the competitive equilibrium within the industry.

The preceding examples touched on the risks associated with production considerations. Those associated with marketing considerations can be just as great. Consider again the sequence of firms A and B exporting from the United States followed by A's establishing a manufacturing subsidiary in country X. By making and selling its products on the scene, A may have a number of marketing advantages over B.

First, A's subsidiary may take on the coloring of a local, not a foreign-controlled, firm, thus reducing the threat to its sales of any nationalistic sentiment against foreign-produced goods. B, of course, has no such protection. Second, A's close proximity to the market place may permit it to tailor its advertising and selling campaigns to local buyer characteristics in ways that B cannot do from a distance. One important consequence of this can be that A so well establishes its trademark or brand name in country X that B has little chance of securing a market franchise even if it should decide to invest locally in order to upgrade its own marketing efforts. Third, because A has its own supply of locally produced goods, it may have advantages in distribution, e.g., regional warehousing, not open to firm B. Alternatively, A may capture all or partial control of a distribution channel essential to the successful marketing of its, and B's, product. B then sells, if at all, at the mercy of A. Finally, if A's and B's products require after-sales servicing, firm A will almost certainly have a competitive edge over B since A has both parts and technicians locally available.

The foregoing list is hardly exhaustive; it presents only a few of the reasons businessmen frequently have cited for "marketing on the scene." Actual surveys of businessmen confirm that marketing considerations have played an important part in foreign investment decisions. For example, Polk, Meister, and Veit (NICB findings) point out that investors are very much concerned with their competitive positions and typically view their direct overseas investments as part of their market strategy:

> Their almost universal reaction is that their investment decisions are made in response to competitive necessities that affect the entire earning position of their operations abroad.
>
> • • • • •
>
> Marketing strategy was found to be not only the overriding consideration in company decisions to undertake production abroad, but often was the controlling factor in determining the form of investment.[11]

Product-pioneering firms, in particular, could be expected to hold this point of view since the essence of their activities has been the discovery and market introduction of new products. Each firm's bundle of capabilities has been only as valuable as its ability to exploit them. Quite naturally, therefore, each product pioneer has tried to guarantee that its ability to "sell" its capabilities has been as great as that of any rival firm.

Now let us consider another set of conditions that may induce oligopolistic reaction. In the case of vertically integrated product-pioneering industries, e.g., aluminum, contest among industry members over sources of supply for minerals or for other raw materials could be expected to prompt checkmating moves by rival firms. To a high degree success in such indus-

---

[11] Judd Polk, Irene W. Meister, and Lawrence A. Veit, *U.S. Production Abroad and the Balance of Payments* (New York: National Industrial Conference Board, 1966), pp. 42 and 60–61.

tries depends on how well firms operate at the extractive and processing stages of production. With respect to operations at these stages, firms try to counterbalance one another not only in terms of costs but also in terms of certainty and reliability of supply. That is, a firm will have the edge over its rivals should it have exclusive access to an especially low-cost source of raw materials or to a source that is much more assured than those available to rivals.

In addition, firms in vertically integrated industries try to make sure that each has about the same number of alternative sources of supply since multiple sources represent protection against the sudden interruption of supply (caused, perhaps, by natural calamity or government interference) from any one country.

If, however, a firm is not matched by its industry rivals and gains a competitive advantage at the extractive or processing stage of production, the risks to its rivals can be far-reaching. The firm with the advantage can capitalize on it throughout its entire integrated manufacturing system and can incorporate its competitive lead, say low material costs, into many products. Moreover, if the firm's operations are integrated across countries, it can pass on its advantage from one country to the next. In short, its threat to rival firms is not isolated; the advantage of the firm can spread out to threaten the worldwide corporate systems of rival firms. In view of this possibility, a matching strategy is obviously a prudent one for vertically integrated firms to adopt.

Summary.—In the last few pages we have considered some of the risks product-pioneering firms could run if the competitive equilibrium in an industry was upset by one firm's gaining a better foothold in a foreign market than that obtained by its industry rivals. Of necessity, the discussion has touched upon only a few of the many different sequences of events that have occurred in the course of U.S. industry's move abroad, and the discussion has identified only a sample of the risks that U.S. firms could face when competitors made direct investments overseas. Nevertheless, it should be clear that when U.S. enterprises established manufacturing subsidiaries abroad, they strengthened their foreign competitive position relative to that of rivals without subsidiaries. Therefore, if a product pioneer did not match the foreign direct investments of its leading rivals, it ran the risk that outside the United States it might not be able to exploit fully its core capabilities. Moreover, this risk might not apply to a single market; the firm's market position might be in jeopardy in a number of foreign countries and even, perhaps, in the United States.

Under the circumstances, firms minimized their risks by matching the foreign direct investments of rivals.[12] Since all the product-pioneering industries were oligopolistic in structure, this risk-minimizing strategy was feasible. Each firm only had to checkmate the moves of a few major rival firms. The strategy guaranteed that no one firm would get an insurmountable upper hand in any industry. And the strategy guaranteed that the costs of perpetuating the oligopolistic equilibrium would be about the same to all rivals in the industry.

As a final note, it is important to re-emphasize that two types of firm behavior, aggressive and defensive, have been discussed here. The product cycle model provides a set of reasons why U.S. product-pioneering firms aggressively pursued for-

---

[12] Here the question arises whether it is reasonable to assume that decisions to undertake direct foreign investments are made in response to oligopolistic pressures. May not some, perhaps many, such decisions be made by top management in response to pressures from corporate subunits—pressures having little to do with the overall economic goals of the firm? The issue this question raises is an adaptation of one of the essential points in Joseph L. Bower, *Managing the Resource Allocation Process* (Boston: Division of Research, Harvard Business School, 1970).

The views and aspirations of middle management undoubtedly have had a bearing upon the decisions of firms to make overseas investments. But this analysis is concerned with the sequence in which direct investments were made and is based upon a sample covering almost 2,000 such investments. It seems highly unlikely therefore that any discernible sequence, one which took on the appearance of a move-countermove pattern, could be accounted for solely on the basis of parochial subunit pressures. And, of course, subunit pressures could be defensive in nature.

eign expansion. Oligopolistic reaction provides a set of reasons why these firms, once caught up in the expansion process, defensively countered the moves of each other to preserve the balance of competitive capabilities within each industry.

The task ahead.—So far it only has been postulated that oligopolistic reaction has been a factor in the overseas expansion of U.S. industry. In the next chapter preliminary findings supporting the premise will be examined. It will be apparent that much of U.S. manufacturing industry has tended to move abroad in lock-step-like fashion. The findings are necessary but hardly sufficient to demonstrate that the foreign investment pattern has been influenced by the desire of U.S. enterprises to perpetuate some sort of oligopolistic equilibrium around the world. Therefore, in the following chapters the investment behavior of U.S. firms is related to firm, industry, and market characteristics to determine if it has been affected by the characteristics in ways generally consistent with the risk-minimizing model just developed.

2

Methodology and Preliminary Findings

I. The Data

The quantitative measure of oligopolistic reaction.—The analytical fulcrum used in this study is a quantitative measure of oligopolistic reaction called "the entry concentration index." The index is a measure of the extent to which U.S. enterprises, by industry, have bunched together the establishment of their foreign manufacturing subsidiaries. A somewhat detailed description of its derivation is necessary, for an understanding of everything else in the pages that follow depends upon an understanding of the measure.

Data sources.—The source of the data for developing the entry concentration indexes (one for each industry: see below) and for some of the statistics used in subsequent chapters to test hypotheses was the "Multinational Enterprise Study." This research project, which has been carried out in two phases since 1966 under the direction of Professor Raymond Vernon of the Harvard Business School, is a comprehensive survey of the international expansion of major U.S.-based and foreign-based corporations. Phase I of the study, which was completed in 1971, covered the history of this expansion, from approximately 1900 through 1967, for 187 large U.S. corporations.[1] Phase II of the study, which was still in progress at the

---

[1] Many of the survey's findings are reviewed in Vernon's *Sovereignty at Bay.* Also, much of the data collected for the Multinational Enterprise Study, in particular data

time of the publication of this book, covers the same topic for 200 non-U.S.-based firms. Phase I culminated in the creation of an extensive data bank; Phase II will do the same.

This study was based on the information contained in the Phase I data bank. The essential facts were: (a) the year in which an overseas subsidiary of a U.S. corporation (the parent firm) was first established, (b) the country in which the subsidiary was located, and (c) the product line of the subsidiary at the time of its formation.

Time period: 1948–1967.—Though data reported in the Multinational Enterprise Study refer to events that took place as far back as, roughly, 1900, in the coming chapters our concern will be with the events that occurred during 1948–1967. There are two reasons for restricting the analysis to this time period. First, with regard to the years before 1946, the available data on industry characteristics at that time were not comprehensive enough to permit testing the associations between these characteristics and the entry concentration indexes. Second, the years 1946–1947 were excluded because it was assumed that during this postwar period the majority of U.S. corporations were concentrating on regrouping and retooling and meeting a high level of domestic demand and thus were not concerned, to any appreciable extent, with such matters as the setting up of foreign subsidiaries.

Countries.—The entry concentration indexes were developed from data on 23 countries within which approximately 83% of all foreign manufacturing subsidiaries of U.S. firms (excluding those in Canada) were established during 1948–1967.[2] Canada was excluded because a number of U.S. firms consider their Canadian operations an integral part of their domestic

---

related to the year, country, and industry in which subsidiaries were established, is reported in James W. Vaupel and Joan P. Curhan, *The Making of Multinational Enterprise* (Boston: Division of Research, Harvard Business School, 1969). Some of the statistical tests for the present analysis incorporate data drawn from this book.

[2] The figure of 83% is based upon data reported in Vaupel and Curhan, *op. cit.*

operations; their reasons therefore for establishing a Canadian subsidiary are not very likely to be the same as their reasons for establishing subsidiaries in other countries. In all other countries that were excluded, the number of subsidiaries by industry was too small for the construction of valid measures of oligopolistic reaction. This is not to say that firms ignored the moves of rivals in these countries (there is, in fact, some evidence of firm interaction), but the data were too fragmentary to be relied upon.

The 23 countries included in the study are:

France	Norway	Peru
Germany	Sweden	Venezuela
Italy	Switzerland	South Africa
Belgium	Spain	Australia
Luxembourg	Argentina	New Zealand
Netherlands	Brazil	Japan
United Kingdom	Colombia	Philippines
Denmark	Mexico	

II. Computation of Entry Concentration Indexes

ECI defined.—An entry concentration index (an ECI) is a quantitative measure of the extent of oligopolistic reaction within a given industry and is based upon the notion that within a limited period of time, the number of subsidiaries U.S. business has established in an industry abroad is an indication of the degree of oligopolistic reaction within that industry.

An ECI is computed for an industrial classification, for an SIC number,[3] and then ranked with other ECIs for other in-

---

[3] The ECIs were computed for three-digit and two-digit industries on the basis of industry classifications defined in the 1963 modified version of the 1957 Standard Industrial Classification Code. For a complete description of the classification system and of the ways in which it has been modified over the years, see U.S. Bureau of the Budget, *Standard Industrial Classification Manual, 1967.*

dustrial classifications, since it is this ranking that gives the number meaning. Thus the term "entry concentration index" means, quite simply, the degree of concentration of the entry (the establishment) of subsidiaries within a specified and limited time period for a given SIC category.[4]

Subsidiaries included in the computation of an ECI.—Only subsidiaries whose principal activity at the time of formation was manufacturing were included in the computations, with the one qualification that those formed as a result of mergers between parent firms were excluded. There were two reasons, both of which reflected limitations on available data, for including only manufacturing subsidiaries. First, the Multinational Enterprise Study gives data on the products or product lines of U.S. manufacturing subsidiaries only; and, second, the same study indicated that the number of nonmanufacturing subsidiaries established during 1948–1967 in many of the 23 countries was so small that it would have been impossible to construct valid measures of oligopolistic reaction for nonmanufacturing industries.

During 1948–1967 in the 23 countries under study some 350 manufacturing subsidiaries were established as the result of mergers of parent firms. These subsidiaries were not included in the sample data, however, because the Multinational Enterprise Study does not identify the dates when the components to the mergers were originally formed. Thus it was not possible to determine whether these subsidiaries were established as countermoves to other subsidiaries or whether they were simply the by-products of various legal steps that were necessary for consolidating the overseas operations of the merging firms or of other decisions having little or nothing to do with oligopolistic reaction.

Computing an ECI.—An illustration of the computation of an ECI—for SIC 283 (Drugs)—will show the process at work.

---

[4] Later we shall see that ECIs can be constructed to provide a measure of entry concentration by country.

When we are determining the ECI for SIC 283, we are concerned with all overseas subsidiaries that manufacture products classified in SIC 283 (restricted, of course, to the 23 countries surveyed and to the years 1948–1967). In a word, the critical factor is the classification of the products of the subsidiary; whether or not its U.S. parent manufactures products classified in SIC 283 is unimportant.

It is entirely possible that a subsidiary manufacturing products in SIC 283 will manufacture other products as well, in, say SIC 284. In this event, the one subsidiary is treated as though it were two and figures into the calculations of the ECIs for both SIC 283 and 284.

The determination of an ECI for SIC 283 involves five simple steps. As a starting point we need the following information for each overseas subsidiary that produces products in SIC 283: (1) the year in which the subsidiary was locally incorporated and (2) the country in which it was established. The second step, then, is to determine the number of subsidiaries that were set up to manufacture products in SIC 283 in each of the 23 countries, in each of the 20 years covered by the study. The third step is to determine, by country, in which three and five and seven consecutive years of the total 20 the largest number of subsidiaries were formed. To make the task easier, since this is an illustration, we shall compute the ECI for only a three-year time period. There are reasons, however, for developing ECIs for all three time periods, and we shall later consider these reasons. Once we have identified the three consecutive years out of the 20 in which the largest number of subsidiaries were formed (in an industry, in a country), the fourth step is to total up the number of subsidiaries (in each industry, in each country) established during this three-year time span. This total, sometimes referred to as "the number of interactions," is the figure we want for each country. For SIC 283 we now have a census of the maximum bunching together of direct investments within three years for each of 23 countries.

The reason data are considered on a country-by-country basis is that the consecutive three-year period of concentrated entry (and the consecutive five-year or seven-year period) was seldom the same for all countries. Chapter 1 pointed out a number of circumstances that could account for this. For example, country A may have imposed restrictions on the importation of drugs in, say, 1951, and U.S. drug manufacturers may have responded by establishing quite a few drug subsidiaries in A in the three years 1952–1954. In contrast, country B may have imposed similar import restrictions in, say, 1962, and U.S. drug manufacturers may have responded by establishing a number of subsidiaries in B in the three years 1963–1965. If, in the cases of both A and B, other direct investments by the U.S. drug industry were few in number and well spread apart in time, then the three-year periods 1952–1954 and 1962–1964 would be identified as those of maximum interactions for A and B respectively.

An ECI is the normalized total of "the largest number" figure for all 23 countries.—Now starting from a position in which we have for each country a figure for the total number of interactions that took place during the three consecutive years in which the largest number of interactions occurred, our final step is to total up these figures and then normalize this total by dividing it by the total of all subsidiaries that were established during the entire 20-year period in all of the 23 countries in which two or more subsidiaries in SIC 283 were formed. This last task is necessary in order to make the ECIs comparable among industries.

Notice that any of the 23 countries in which fewer than two subsidiaries in SIC 283 were formed were excluded from all the calculations. This exclusion follows from the basic notion that an ECI is a reflection of the interactions among subsidiaries; thus in the case of countries in which there was one or no subsidiary in SIC 283, there was of course no interaction.

For a simple model of the process of constructing an ECI, see Table 2-1.

TABLE 2-1

Simplified Example of the Construction of an ECI
(hypothetical data for SIC 283)

	Year										Maximum No. of Subsidiaries in Any 3 Consecutive Years	Total No. Subsidiaries Formed
	1	2	3	4	5	6	7	8	9	10		
Entry into Country A: Subs. manufacturing in SIC 283 & formed in year indicated	3	5	5	2	1	2	2	1	1	1	13	23
Entry into Country B: Subs. manufacturing in SIC 283 & formed in year indicated	3	1	1	3	4	2	1	1	1	1	9	18
Total: Countries A & B											22	41

$$\text{Three-year Entry Concentration Index} = \frac{\text{Maximum 3 Consecutive Years}}{\text{Total Subsidiaries Formed}}$$

$$= \frac{22}{41} = .538$$

Three-year, five-year, seven-year, and average ECIs.—For each three-digit industry three-year, five-year, and seven-year ECIs were computed, and all three were used in the statistical tests. It was necessary to do this because the choice concerning the number of consecutive years to be used in computing the ECIs was an arbitrary one and because it was entirely possible that too short or too long a time span would introduce bias into the analysis.

The example cited above of investment in countries A and B by U.S. drug manufacturers can be used to clarify the difference between a three-year ECI and five-year and seven-year ECIs. In the example, during 1948–1967 the largest number of subsidiaries ever established within any three consecutive years in A and B were set up in 1952–1954 and in

1963–1965 respectively. Suppose, however, our concern is the largest number established in five consecutive years. Then the data might show, for instance, that the maximum bunching in A and B took place in 1952–1956 and 1963–1967. That is, the relevant five-year periods start with the same years as the three-year periods but extend for two more years. Or, if the U.S. drug industry invested in each country in two different surges, it could be that the maximum bunching within five consecutive years occurred in time periods unrelated to the three-year time spans. Thus the notion of a consecutive number of years (for one industry in one country) holds for all the ECIs, but the concept does not necessarily require that the same years will be included in each ECI.

In addition to the three-year, five-year, and seven-year ECIs, an average ECI was determined for each three-digit industry. It is the simple average of an industry's three-year, five-year, and seven-year ECIs, and it is used as a general measure of the concentration of subsidiary formation by industry. In most of the statistical tests performed, all four ECIs were used, since the relationships between the three-year ECI of a given industry and other variables descriptive of the industry were seldom the same as the relationships between the descriptive variables and the industry's five-year or seven-year ECIs.

Appendix A lists the values of the ECIs for all industries for which ECIs could be computed.

ECIs by country.—The procedure used for computing the ECIs by industry may also be used, with one adjustment, for computing ECIs by country. Whereas industry ECIs are calculated by adding up by industry and across countries the largest number of interactions within specified time spans, country ECIs are calculated by adding up by countries and across industries the largest number of interactions within specified time spans. Thus, starting from a position in which we have the largest number of interactions for each time span (for each industry and each country), we add up these figures for *all* industries by each country and normalize the totals by dividing them by the total number of interactions that took place in the countries during the entire 20-year period. Then when three-year, five-year, and seven-year ECIs have been computed for each country, a simple average of these three will give us an average ECI by country.

Appendix B lists the values of the ECIs for all countries for which ECIs could be computed.

Product proliferation within existing subsidiaries: a problem? —The reader who has patiently followed the details in the last few pages may object at this point that the computation of the ECIs ignores an occurrence that could significantly affect their validity. The problem perceived would be the following. The ECIs are based *solely* on subsidiaries' three-digit product lines as of the time when the subsidiaries were first established in foreign countries. But, after that point in time, subsidiaries could manufacture any number of new three-digit product lines. Consequently, product proliferation within existing sub-sidiaries, in addition to setting up new subsidiaries, might have been a common way by which U.S. firms countered the over-seas moves of rivals. And if this were true, the ECIs would be quite incomplete measures of oligopolistic reaction.

Fortunately, it is possible to answer this objection, though not in a completely satisfactory way. The data of the Multina-tional Enterprise Study do not indicate the year established subsidiaries added new three-digit product lines. But the data do indicate the complete three-digit product lines of all foreign manufacturing subsidiaries as of 1966. From these data two facts can be determined: (1) some product proliferation did take place, but (2) the extent of the proliferation was surpris-ingly low.

In all the subsidiaries included in the sample, those formed in the 23 countries and 20 years of interest, only 125 new three-digit product lines were added between the time the sub-sidiaries were initially established and 1966. Compared to the total number of three-digit products manufactured in all the sampled subsidiaries as of 1966, the new products amounted to no more than 5%.

Moreover, product proliferation was not concentrated by country or by industry. In 18 of the 23 countries, subsidiaries added products subsequent to their formation, and the new products fell in almost all of the three-digit industries under study. Since, relative to the total number of three-digit products used in the ECI calculations, the number of unrecorded new products was so small, and since these additions were spread out over so many countries and industries, it seemed safe to assume that their absence from the data base did not introduce any systematic bias.

One specific test confirmed this assumption. Once established, more subsidiaries subsequently added products in SIC 282 (Plastics Materials and Synthetics) than in any other three-digit industry. Because data on when these additions took place were not available, it was necessary to assume the date of their occurrence to test what effect they might have had on the value of SIC 282's ECIs. On the supposition that these products were introduced within the three-year, five-year, and seven-year periods identified to create the actual ECIs for SIC 282, revised ECIs for the industry were calculated. The difference between the actual and the revised ECIs was minimal. In effect, the rank order of the values of the ECIs for SIC 282 shifted up one place in the list of all the ECIs computed for this study. (See Appendix A for a complete list of ECIs.) Clearly, if product proliferation in the industry where it was most intense makes so little difference in the values of the ECIs, proliferation in other industries should have a negligible effect on their values.

III. Industries Included or Excluded from Analysis

Industries excluded.—The Standard Industrial Classification Code lists 141 three-digit manufacturing industries, which fall within 20 two-digit SIC manufacturing categories. ECIs, however, could be computed for only 54 of the 141 three-digit industries, all of which fell within 12 of the 20 two-digit industries. This limitation in the data came about because a number of U.S. manufacturing industries at the three-digit level either have not established subsidiaries overseas, or have so scattered these among countries that the number of interactions within the same country during the 20-year period was negligible.

SIC 22 (Textile Mill Products), for instance, was excluded because only a few interactions took place within that industry. Two firms in SIC 222, two in SIC 229, and two in SIC 228 established competing manufacturing subsidiaries; but in the case of the first two industries interactions were confined to a single country, and in the case of SIC 228, interactions occurred in only three countries.

Six other two-digit industries (see below) were excluded because the available data indicated that in no instance did two or more U.S. parent firms belonging to the same industry establish competing manufacturing subsidiaries in the same country in the same overseas industry. These two-digit industries were:

SIC Code	Industry Title
21	Tobacco Manufacturers
23	Apparel & Other Textile Products
24	Lumber & Wood Products
25	Furniture & Fixtures
27	Printing & Publishing
31	Leather & Leather Products

And finally, SIC 39 (Miscellaneous Manufacturing Industries) was excluded because only a few interactions took place within this industry, all of which were confined to a few three-digit industries; and the miscellaneous nature of its three-digit industries made it virtually impossible to make assumptions about any competitive reaction that might have taken place within them.

Two characteristics of the excluded industries.—That the eight two-digit industries discussed above had to be excluded from analysis for want of sufficient data is an important point in itself. It is the first bit of evidence corroborating the conceptual scheme laid out in Chapter 1. For two reasons the member firms in these industries seldom engaged in foreign direct investment.

First, by almost any standard, the member firms would not be regarded as product pioneers. True, styling and craftsmanship may be prerequisites for product success in such industries as textiles and furniture, but still one would not regard the products of these industries as characterized by high innovational content. Certainly these are not industries one associates with high levels of R&D activity. Moreover, small scale, not large scale, typifies manufacturing operations in most of the eight industries. In short, of all manufacturing industries, these eight are the farthest removed from the model of product-pioneering industries.

Second, of the eight industries excluded from analysis, all but one are non-oligopolistic in structure. Establishing this point as fact calls for a brief discussion of a standard measure of industry structure, the industry concentration ratio. This ratio, which is the percentage of total industry sales accounted for by a specified number (usually 4 or 8) of the leading firms in an industry, is commonly regarded as an indicator of oligopoly structure. When, for instance, the ratio for an industry is high, the industry is conventionally thought of as being highly oligopolistic.

Now, for seven of the eight excluded industries the eight-firm concentration ratio (see Appendix C for a description of its computation) is low, falling in the 20% to 40% range. In contrast, the value of this ratio for the 12 industries included in the analysis (see next section) falls generally in the 40% to 80% range. Clearly, high industry concentration is positively linked to foreign direct investment. The one exception mentioned above, which happens to be the tobacco industry, merits comment. The industry is highly concentrated; the leading few firms account for 100% of industry sales. Moderate to large scale, in terms of both production and marketing, commonly prevails in the industry. The tobacco manufacturers excel at establishing brand names. Thus, according to the criteria spelled out in Chapter 1, we would expect that they would be active foreign direct investors. Why has this not been the case?

Certainly one reason tobacco manufacturers have stayed at home has been their inability to enter a number of foreign markets where government monopolies controlled the tobacco industry. Another reason has been that they developed few capabilities exploitable in markets outside the United States. Their technological skills were not exceptional and were quite industry specific. And the one asset U.S. tobacco manufacturers might have exploited abroad, their brand names, were not of much use because European competitors had thoroughly established their own brand names by the turn of the century.

The international expansion of the Philip Morris company is the one exception that tends to prove the rule. Philip Morris, in contrast to its principal U.S. competitors, was originally a British firm. Only in 1919 was the company taken over by a group of U.S. investors. Yet, as one of its executives observed, the firm had a historical basis for international expansion:

> Being a British company in the days of the Empire, the Philip Morris name had been established around the world; it was in a sense an international company from the outset. Unlike some of our competitors, our domestic brand names belonged to us overseas as well.[5]

When, beginning in the 1950s, Philip Morris started to establish foreign subsidiaries, it did so to exploit brand names long familiar to smokers in overseas markets. Thus the one U.S. tobacco manufacturer actively engaged in foreign direct investment profited from capabilities like those of other product-pioneering firms.

---

[5] The quote and information on Philip Morris are taken from Philip Morris Incorporated, Harvard Business School Case 4-372-045, 1971.

In summary, eight two-digit industries have been excluded from further analysis because the member firms in the industries traditionally paid little attention to investment abroad. Their inattention to overseas opportunities appears to be related to the fact that they did not develop capabilities that could be exploited in foreign markets and to the fact that they did not (with the exception noted) operate under oligopoly conditions.

Industries included in the analysis.—In the pages ahead we shall be concerned with only those 12 two-digit industries that encompass the 54 three-digit industries under analysis, and the 12 will be referred to simply as "the 12 international industries" or as "the 12 international two-digit industries." They are listed in Table 2-2. Even at a glance, it is clear that these 12 industries differ from the eight excluded from analysis. In one way or another each of the 12 matches the description of a product-pioneering industry. And, according to their concentration ratios, most are oligopolistic in structure.

TABLE 2-2

The Twelve International Two-Digit Industries

SIC Code	Industry Title	Eight-Firm Concentration Ratio*
20	Food and Kindred Products	48.2%
26	Paper and Allied Products	47.0
28	Chemicals and Allied Products	60.7
29	Petroleum and Coal Products	55.9
30	Rubber and Plastics Products	64.7
32	Stone, Clay, and Glass Products	74.3
33	Primary Metal Industries	65.9
34	Fabricated Metal Products	38.9
35	Machinery, Except Electrical	53.7
36	Electrical Equipment and Supplies	62.0
37	Transportation Equipment	80.6
38	Instruments and Related Products	59.2

* The reader is referred to Appendix C for a description of the computation of these ratios.

This second point is, to be sure, hardly a new finding. Many authors have observed that almost all U.S. foreign direct investments are made by firms that are part of oligopolies in the United States and that these firms tend to invest abroad in industries that are also oligopolistic in structure.[6] With one or two exceptions, these observations were based, like the one above, on the study of industry concentration data. Stephen Hymer's evidence is typical:

> It appears that 44 percent of the principal U.S. foreign investors come from industries where four firms supply over three-fourths of sales, although these industries account for only eight percent of total value of industrial output in the United States. By contrast, industries where the four largest firms provide less than one-fourth of sales had only one of the seventy-two firms classified as major foreign investors.[7]

The data in Table 2-2, while they confirm the observations of others, still do not demonstrate that oligopolistic reaction has been a major force compelling U.S. firms in the 12 industries to invest abroad. Static industry concentration data do not permit the determination of the existence or nonexistence

---

[6] See, for instance, Jack N. Behrman, *Some Patterns in the Rise of the Multinational Enterprise* (Chapel Hill: Graduate School of Business Administration, University of North Carolina, 1969); Donald T. Brash, *American Investment in Australian Industry* (Cambridge: Harvard University Press, 1966); John H. Dunning, *American Investment in the British Manufacturing Industry* (London: George Allen and Unwin Ltd., 1958); John H. Dunning, *The Role of American Investment in the British Economy* (London: P.E.P., 1969); Stephen Hymer, "The International Operations of National Firms—A Study of Direct Foreign Investment" (unpublished doctoral dissertation, M.I.T., 1960); E. A. Safarian, *Foreign Ownership of Canadian Industry* (New York: McGraw-Hill Book Company, 1966); William Gruber, Dileep Mehta, and Raymond Vernon, "The R&D Factor in International Trade and International Investment of United States Industries," *Journal of Political Economy*, Vol. LXXV, No. 1 (February 1967) (reprinted in Louis T. Wells, Jr. (ed.), *The Product Life Cycle and International Trade*. Boston: Division of Research, Harvard Business School, 1972).

[7] Stephen Hymer, "Direct Foreign Investment and International Oligopoly" (1965 mimeo.), cited in Bela Balassa, "American Direct Investment in the Common Market," *Banca Nazionale del Lavoro Quarterly Review* (June 1966), p. 124.

of oligopolistic reaction. Up to this point it has simply been established that the industries that will be of interest to us are those that fit the conceptual model spelled out in Chapter 1.

IV. An Underlying Pattern

Overall entry concentration.—Once the ECIs are computed, they may be used in various ways, and in this sense they are a tool for analysis. When, for example, the interactions that took place during the time spans used in analysis (three, five, or seven consecutive years) are summed in all 54 industries, and this figure is then expressed as a percentage of the total number of interactions that took place within these industries during the entire 20-year period, we have an indication of the overall propensity of firms to bunch together their foreign direct investments.

The basic statistical data show that during the 20 years under study a total of 1,892 interactions took place within all 54 industries, and that 878 of these interactions, or 46%, took place in clusters within three-year time spans. Since these data and those that follow in the next several paragraphs are easily subject to misinterpretation, it is necessary to re-emphasize again just what is and is not being measured by the ECIs.

The data *do not* show that 46% of all subsidiaries set up during 1948–1967 in all 54 industries were established within the same three years. That is, the data do not show that 46% of all the subsidiaries were formed, irrespective of industry, in any one three-year period, say, for instance, 1958–1960. Nor do the data show that U.S. parent firms established their subsidiaries within the same three-year periods in one country after another, e.g., *all* parent firms made 46% of their investments in country A in 1956–1958 and 46% of their investments in country B in 1961–1963.

What the data do show is that for each of the 54 industries within each individual country, direct investments have tended to be clustered together. When clusters are measured over any three consecutive years during 1948–1967, when the *peak* cluster is identified for each industry, country by country, and when the numbers of subsidiaries included in each peak cluster, for all industries and countries, are added up and compared with the total number of subsidiaries established in the years under study, the figures show that 46% of all subsidiaries were formed in the three-year clusters.

This clustering of investments can, of course, be measured over periods other than three-year spans, and this is just what the five-year and seven-year ECIs do. The data further show that 1,179 interactions, or 62%, occurred in five-year clusters and 1,411 interactions, or 75%, occurred within seven-year clusters. Naturally, all of the usual qualifications must accompany these figures, since they apply only to the subsidiaries under consideration.

We now have some empirical findings that suggest that the foreign direct investments of U.S. business have been bunched together. Yet the reader may have some misgivings about these findings, questioning their validity on at least two counts.

First, the reader might contend, the overall trend of U.S. direct investments abroad, particularly the surge in the early 1960s, may have created a compact pattern of investments. The wave of investments need not have been related to the desire of firms to counter one another's investments. But because data on the investments were probably included in the ECI calculations, clustering, erroneously interpreted as evidence of oligopolistic reaction, could be the result. In short, U.S. industry's expansion abroad, in the aggregate and regardless of motivation, may have produced the observed bunching of investments.

Second, what the ECIs indicate as clustered investments in each industry could be in actuality the results of haphazard arrangements of events. That is, ECIs calculated from randomized subsidiary formations may not be statistically different from the actual ECIs.

It is best to acknowledge these two methodological problems

now when they first become apparent. It will be more useful, however, to set them at rest at the end of the next chapter after the critically important statistical results of that chapter have been discussed. Then, tests employing randomly generated ECIs will establish the extent to which one can be confident of the validity of all the preceding findings.

V. Four Specific Points on Methodology

Terminology.—So far as concepts and terms are concerned, most of those we shall be dealing with in the coming chapters are used in studies of industrial organization and corporate strategy. Similarly, almost all the empirical tests will be based upon methodological techniques commonly used in the field of industrial organization.

A few topics will be treated from the point of view of the theory of games and the theory of conflict; but analytical techniques associated with game theory, though they have been used by others to investigate firm behavior under conditions of oligopoly, will not be used principally because these techniques were developed for theoretical analyses and this is an empirical study.

Statistical methodology.—Many of the statistical analyses ahead were based upon simple correlations, even though multiple regression would have been a more efficient and powerful tool for getting the job done. Multiple regression was used only twice, however, mainly because important limitations on available data precluded its effective use more often.

When the statistical data were based exclusively upon industrial structure or industrial activity within the United States, regressing the ECIs on a number of statistical series would have been possible. But when the statistical series for the independent variables were based on a mixed bag of data covering industrial activity both abroad and in the United States, the constantly shifting data bases made the use of regression analysis impossible. Hence simple correlations were employed in all but two cases because they permitted the use of the "best data."

Industry and market characteristics and entry concentration. —With one exception, the effects on entry concentration of industry characteristics and of market characteristics were dealt with separately. This seemingly unrealistic separation—industry and market characteristics are undoubtedly interrelated in some industries—requires an explanation. Why, for instance, was the research not directed at examining entry concentration by industry, by country?

First, data specific to a given industry in a given country were seldom available for all the industries and countries under study. And such data would be necessary for an analysis of the joint effects of industry and market characteristics on entry concentration.

Second, to be meaningful the data in the 23-country by 54-industry by 20-year matrix had to be aggregated. Only after interactions were combined across industries and across countries, resulting in ECIs by country and by industry, did patterns begin to emerge that suggested the existence of relationships between entry concentration and other variables.

Level of industry classification.—There are certain problems associated with using one level of industry classification instead of another. This point can be made clear if we consider the matter from the standpoint of the findings of Professor Robert Stobaugh, who analyzed foreign direct investments in the petrochemical industry. Stobaugh, using data on nine petrochemical products, all of which were identified at roughly the five-digit SIC level and classified in SIC 281 (Industrial Chemicals), found no evidence that oligopolistic reaction induced foreign direct investments in the petrochemical industry.[8]

---

[8] Stobaugh, in his analysis, traced the history of international investment in manufacturing plants set up to produce petrochemicals and found no instance, within a pe-

In contrast, the empirical finding of the present analysis (see Appendix A) is that some oligopolistic reaction (though admittedly not a great deal) did occur in SIC 281. The disparity between the two findings raises several questions; and as in the case of many comparisons of this kind, the qualifications associated with each finding often account for the difference.

Stobaugh's conclusion that oligopolistic reaction was of no importance in the petrochemical industry was based upon statistical data specific to one segment of SIC 281. Moreover, the nine petrochemical products he surveyed represented only 10% or so of the total output of SIC 281.[9]

Now when we compare Stobaugh's finding with the average ECI for SIC 281, which was in the bottom quartile of all average ECIs, the first point of interest is that both findings suggest the possibility that oligopolistic reaction in the petrochemical industry—if it took place at all—was of some low level of magnitude. And this raises the question whether the disparities noted are mainly the result of differences in the levels of industry classification that were used in the two studies.

Recall that the present analysis is based upon data classified at the three-digit and two-digit SIC level, whereas Stobaugh was concerned with products classified at the five-digit SIC level. It can be argued, therefore, that if the cross-elasticities of demand and the cross-elasticities of supply among the nine petrochemicals, classified at the five-digit level, were very low, competition among the firms producing these petrochemicals would have occurred in nine distinct markets, and Stobaugh's conclusion would necessarily follow.

---

riod of five consecutive years, when two or more firms established plants in the same foreign country to manufacture the same petrochemical. This finding, although it relates to only a small portion of Stobaugh's research on the petrochemical industry, is of special significance as far as the present research is concerned because Stobaugh's approach to measuring oligopolistic reaction is the father of the entry concentration index. See Robert B. Stobaugh, Jr., "The Product Life Cycle, U. S. Exports, and International Investment" (unpublished doctoral dissertation, Harvard Business School, 1968).

[9] Ten percent is Professor Stobaugh's estimate.

But suppose, on the other hand, that for any of a number of reasons, a buyer of petrochemicals would be perfectly willing to substitute petrochemical A for petrochemical B. Then one could argue that if the establishment of a plant in a given country for the production of chemical A were followed within a few years by the establishment in the same country of a plant for the production of chemical B, this could be a case of oligopolistic reaction.

Stobaugh, though he believes there was no cross-elasticity of supply among the nine petrochemicals, acknowledges at the present time that there might have been some cross-elasticity of demand. In any event, one could argue that Stobaugh's conclusion, based as it was on a methodology similar to that used in this study, was determined by the fine level of industry classification of his data; and had his data, along with his methodology, been similar to that used in the present analysis, then his finding too would have closely approximated that of this research.

3

Industry Structure

and Oligopolistic Reaction

I. The Hypothesis

The preceding chapters discharged two essential tasks. Chapter 1 furnished the reasons for expecting that product-pioneering oligopolists, in order to perpetuate competitive equilibrium, would checkmate each other's overseas investments. Chapter 2 established that product-pioneering oligopolists have, in fact, moved abroad in close-order fashion. Now, we are ready to consider the first body of evidence that directly supports the notion that oligopolistic reaction has had a part in the clustering of foreign direct investments.

The evidence is the result of an examination of the relationship between two variables: one a measure of oligopolistic reaction, and the other a measure of industry structure. This relationship was investigated because it was hypothesized that for U.S. industries involved in international expansion after World War II, the higher the concentration of output of the leading firms in a given industry, the higher that industry's level of oligopolistic reaction. In other words, firms in highly concentrated industries should have matched competitors' foreign investments more closely than did firms in less concentrated industries. Why expect such a relationship between industry structure and firm behavior?

Industry concentration and firm behavior.—The link between industry concentration and firm behavior is, at least theoretically, a quite simple one. The more concentrated an industry, the more obvious it will be to management of each leading firm that its success depends not only on its own acts but upon the acts of its rivals. Higher industry concentration, therefore, produces more interdependent firm behavior. When two firms dominate an industry, neither can ignore for long what the other is doing. When, on the other hand, eight firms dominate an industry, assuming that all eight share the market about equally, each can discount somewhat the moves of a rival. The effect of one firm's moves, spread over the remaining seven firms, may seem to represent only a minor competitive hazard to each individual industry member.

This simple structure-behavior relationship can be extended to apply to export sales and foreign direct investment. The example, although elementary, provides one illustration of why increasing industry concentration should be positively associated with increasing entry concentration.

Assume that two rival U.S. manufacturers, A and B, each export $50 million of goods to a foreign market. Now suppose that A establishes a subsidiary in the export market, and, as a result of manufacturing and marketing on the scene, A increases its sales by 10% at the expense of B's exports. Unless B makes a compensatory move, it suffers a loss of 10% of export sales.

In contrast to the preceding situation where export sales were concentrated, assume now that five U.S. manufacturers, A through E, supply the same foreign market, each firm having $20 million in export sales. Assume further that A puts up a plant in the export market and, for the reasons mentioned in the first case, experiences a 10% gain in sales at the expense of B through E. Again, unless firms B through E counter in some way, they suffer a loss in export sales. But for each the loss is only roughly 2.5% of export sales.

Now, it seems entirely reasonable to expect that firm B in the first case will view A's move abroad as more threatening than firms B through E in the second case will view their rival's move abroad. Moreover, it seems reasonable to expect that B in the first case will more actively try to counterbalance its rival than B through E will try to counterbalance their rival. If counterbalancing takes the form of matching direct investments, then entry concentration (as it is measured in this study) should be higher in the first of the two cases.

Of course, this hypothetical illustration could be objected to on a number of grounds. It could be argued, for instance, that the degree of concentration of export sales may bear little or no relation to the degree of industry concentration in domestic or foreign markets. For large rival manufacturers it would seem that interdependency is more likely to depend on the structure of their industry at home or abroad than on any one export situation. Yet the history of product-pioneering industries suggests that there probably has been a positive association between industry concentration in the United States and concentration in export sales. Recall that the product-pioneering oligopolists have been the leading exporters of manufactured goods. Thus a few firms in each product-pioneering industry have dominated export sales as they have dominated home sales. It follows that any sense of interdependency that evolved among rival product pioneers at home could have been carried over into their export operations.

It should be noted that the export example cited above is presented for illustrative purposes only. Certainly high levels of domestic industry concentration could produce interdependent foreign investment behavior among rival product pioneers even if none had export sales. That is, regardless of how they might exploit overseas their unique capabilities, product pioneers most likely have struggled to protect the future international earnings potential of their capabilities in the same way that they have skirmished to protect market share at home. And the fewer the number of firms commanding the capabilities (the more concentrated the industry), the greater the future earnings potential of the capabilities to any one firm; hence, the more intense the contest to protect their future exploitability.

Qualifying the hypothesis.—The general hypothesis, that entry concentration has been positively related to industry concentration, must be qualified in one important way. There are reasons to believe that at very high levels of industry concentration rivalry has tended to become less intense, rather than more intense. Constrained rivalry in industries dominated by very few firms explains why this probably has been the case.

When only two or three firms supplied all of an industry's output, and after they made their few initial direct investments overseas, the diseconomies involved in their all following a countering strategy may have become quite apparent to them. If each promptly matched the direct investments of the other, the result, they could see, could be injury to all. By bunching their direct investments together, they may have established manufacturing capacity far in excess of what the local market could absorb. If this were the case, then, at least in the short run, each firm was saddled with unprofitable facilities. Then too, if they bunched their direct investments together, in some markets they may have had to compete for an insufficient supply of factor inputs. When U.S. investors first set up plants abroad, it was not uncommon for them to find that raw materials, component parts, and trained personnel were in short supply or were inappropriate for the needs of the plants. Even though these deficiencies could be corrected over time, the problems may have been exacerbated when several U.S. investors were trying to do so at the same time.

Deficiencies could also exist on the marketing side. For instance, the distribution systems in some markets may have been inadequate or insufficiently sophisticated to handle the goods produced by U.S. subsidiaries. When several product pioneers invested abroad in one country at about the same time, their near simultaneous drive to expand their selling efforts could overtax the local marketing system. Again, it could be a case of too many entrants all at one time.

To be sure, the disadvantages of clustering together direct investments would also crop up when the member firms in loose oligopolies moved abroad in close-order fashion. But there is a difference between the situation when only two or three firms in an industry were investing abroad and the situation when a number of firms, say six, seven, or eight rivals, were investing abroad. In the first case, the interdependency of their acts, the damage that each could do to the others by investing on the heels of one another, would be obvious. Consequently, they might arrive at an understanding (explicit or implicit) that they would all benefit if they spaced out, either in time or over countries, their investments. In the second case, the interdependency of their acts would be less obvious. More importantly, the likelihood of establishing and maintaining some sort of understanding to "rationalize" the pattern of their investments would not be high. In short, self-imposed constraint among two or three firms was a possibility; self-imposed constraint among seven or eight rivals was another matter.

Summing up, if oligopolistic reaction was a feature of the foreign investment behavior of U.S. firms, the tendency to counter industry rivals' moves should have increased with increasing industry concentration. In quite highly concentrated industries, however, the relationship was probably the reverse. The evidence about to be examined bears out these conjectures. First, however, it is necessary to explain how the evidence was generated.

The measures.—The measure of oligopolistic reaction that was used was the entry concentration index (the ECI). Bear in mind that the use of the ECI depends upon one fundamental assumption: the higher an industry's ECI, the higher the level of oligopolistic reaction within that industry.

The measure of industry structure that was used was the industry concentration ratio: that part of an industry's total output that is produced and sold by the leading four or eight or n firms in an industry and which is expressed as the n-firm concentration ratio.[1] If, for instance, the collective output of the

---

[1] The source of data for these ratios was U.S. Senate, Subcommittee on Antitrust and Monopoly of the Committee on the Judiciary, *Concentration Ratios in Manufacturing Industry 1963*, 89th Cong., 2d Sess., 1966. *(Footnote 1 continued on p. 58)*

four largest firms in an industry is 80% of total industry output, then the four-firm concentration ratio for that industry will be 80%.

The industry concentration ratio, though a standard analytical tool of economists, is not without statistical and theoretical shortcomings.[2] Difficulties in classifying manufacturers by distinct industries detract from the ratio's usefulness. Two features of modern industrial activity—product innovation leading to substitute products and product diversification leading to alternative sources of supply—make it difficult, frequently impossible, to identify distinct industries.

In addition, as an index of market power the industry concentration ratio falls short of the mark because it does not measure, except indirectly, certain industrial characteristics, such as barriers to entry, that also create market power.

Criticisms like these rest on solid ground. Yet the fact remains that the industry concentration ratio is a productive tool, and its shortcomings need not negate its usefulness if we are aware of what these shortcomings are and where they might influence certain findings.

In order to have a broadly based but not too general measure of industry structure, the eight-firm concentration ratio was employed routinely in statistical tests. On a few occasions, however, the four-firm concentration ratio was used when the purpose was to determine if observed relationships were the result of the behavior of only the leading few firms in each industry.

As is frequently the case, the inevitable difficulties and

(Footnote 1 continued)

The use of 1963 U.S. industry concentration ratios as the sole measure of industry structure opens this research to criticism on two counts. First, whereas the concentration ratios relate only to the year 1963, the ECIs are based on subsidiary formations that occurred sometime during 1948–1967. Second, U.S. concentration ratios may be poor indicators of the level of industrial concentration in foreign countries. These criticisms are dealt with in statistical tests that are discussed in Appendix D; and although such criticisms cannot be dismissed entirely, the evidence indicates that they point out relatively inconsequential weaknesses in the data.

[2] For a review of the shortcomings of the industry concentration ratio see the introductory textual material in *Concentration Ratios in Manufacturing Industry 1963.*

shortcomings in data made minor data adjustments necessary. Appendix C describes these adjustments in detail; only their principal features will be noted here.

Because many of the published sources of information dealing with international business, particularly those of the U.S. Government, present data at the SIC two-digit industry level only, both the ECIs and the industry concentration ratios were, for the purposes of some tests, aggregated to that level of industry classification. In the case of the industry concentration ratios, which are reported by the Bureau of the Census at the four-digit industry level only, data were aggregated to successively higher levels of industry classification by weighting each industry's ratio by the value of its U.S. shipments. In the case of the ECIs the procedure was more complex and varied somewhat among industries. The reader is referred to Appendix D.

Also, in order to ensure complete comparability with the ECIs, some industries were dropped from the computation of the concentration ratios. For example, the ECI for SIC 30, the rubber industry, was based only on the underlying ECIs for SICs 301, 302, 303, and 306. For consistency the industry concentration ratio for SIC 30 was based on the data for the same four three-digit industries. Throughout the remainder of this study concentration ratios are usually referred to as adjusted to remind the reader that the data are not in their raw form.

II. Correlation Results

An overview of the findings.—Various correlations between the two variables discussed in the preceding section served the useful purpose of getting the analysis under way. They constituted the first hesitant steps into new territory. Once they revealed a set of positive relationships between entry concentration and industry concentration and, more importantly, once they helped make understandable the nature of the relationships, analysis could be refined through the use of the regression technique to determine if the association between the variables was in fact nonlinear. But let us consider the findings one step at a time.

Three statements summarize the import of the correlation results about to be examined. One, entry concentration, the bunching together of foreign direct investments, has been positively associated with industry concentration. Two, the positive association observed between the two variables seems to have been the result of the behavior of a few leading firms in each industry. And three, entry concentration has tended to be most intense in industries in which marketing capabilities, above all else, have been the key to success.

The individual findings are not entirely unambiguous, but considered all together, they clearly support the three relationships just described.

Correlation of ECIs and eight-firm concentration ratios at the three-digit industry level.

—The first step in determining the relationship between entry concentration and industry concentration was correlation of ECIs for 34 three-digit industries with the values of the corresponding adjusted eight-firm concentration ratios. Only three-digit industries in which ten or more interactions took place were included in the correlations, i.e., those with ECIs based on exceptionally small samples were excluded.[3] Likewise, all three-digit industries with SIC codes ending in nine were excluded; since these consist of miscellaneous industries lumped together, it was impossible to make assumptions about the competitive reactions of firms in these industries.

For the 34 three-digit industries included in the sample, Pearson and Spearman correlations gave the results shown in Table 3-1.

---

[3] This exclusion did not bias the test in one way or the other. The average values of the 20 ECIs excluded, those ECIs based on exceptionally small samples, were slightly higher than the average values of the ECIs included. But, as one would expect with small samples, the standard deviations for the excluded ECIs were much larger, generally twice as large, as those for the included ECIs.

TABLE 3-1

Coefficients of Correlation of ECIs with Adjusted Eight-Firm Concentration Ratios for Three-Digit Industries
(N = 34)

	Pearson r	Spearman r
3-year ECI	+.27 (.064)[a]	+.22 (.111)
5-year ECI	+.41 (.008)	+.32 (.030)
7-year ECI	+.31 (.038)	+.18 (.153)
Average ECI	+.38 (.014)	+.22 (.101)

[a] In this and in almost all the statistical tables that follow, the result of the normal one-tailed test for statistical significance is reported in parentheses after each coefficient. Though this is not the conventional way of handling the matter, it is done here because it gives the reader an indication, along with what is provided by the coefficients, of how relationships between variables and ECIs change from one ECI to the next.

Correlation of ECIs and eight-firm concentration ratios at the two-digit industry level.—When the ECIs and concentration ratios were aggregated to the two-digit industry level, correlation between these two variables gave equivocal results as may be seen in Table 3-2.

TABLE 3-2

Coefficients of Correlation of ECIs with Adjusted Eight-Firm Concentration Ratios for Two-Digit Industries
(N = 12)

	Pearson r	Spearman r
3-year ECI	+.51 (.047)	+.43 (.080)
5-year ECI	+.05 (.443)	+.10 (.373)
7-year ECI	−.09 (.389)	−.08 (.398)
Average ECI	+.25 (.218)	+.15 (.317)

With the exception of the three-year ECI, the relationship between entry concentration and industry concentration, at least at the two-digit industry level, was inconclusive. Three features of the data at the two-digit industry level may account for these results. First, aggregating the ECIs to the two-digit level did not improve intercorrelation among the ECIs. Inter-correlation of the ECIs at the three-digit level produced about the same results as intercorrelation at the two-digit level. Table 3-3 shows, at the two-digit level, the coefficients of inter-correlation among the ECIs. Keep in mind that in view of the low level of intercorrelation among the ECIs, there need be no inherent contradiction in our finding on the one hand a posi-tive correlation between the three-year ECI and industry con-centration and on the other hand no correlation between the five-year or seven-year ECIs and industry concentration ra-tios.

TABLE 3-3

**Pearson Coefficients of Intercorrelation of ECIs
for Two-Digit Industries**
(N = 12)

	3-year ECI	5-year ECI	7-year ECI	Average ECI
3-year ECI	+1.00 (.001)	+ .60 (.020)	+ .42 (.086)	+ .85 (.001)
5-year ECI		+1.00 (.001)	+ .73 (.004)	+ .90 (.001)
7-year ECI			+1.00 (.001)	+ .78 (.001)
Average ECI				+1.00 (.001)

Notice the high positive correlations between the average ECI and the ECIs for each of the three time periods. At cer-tain points in this study, when it was necessary to make statis-tical tests at the two-digit industry level, the average ECI was sometimes used alone.

A second feature of the data at the two-digit industry level that may account for the inconclusive results concerns SIC 30. The relationship between the ECIs and the concentration ra-tios for the industries at the two-digit level became clearer when data for SIC 30—that is, the combined interactions in SICs 301–303 and 306—were excluded. SIC 30, the rubber in-dustry, kept reappearing in the data as an anomaly. Later in this study we shall look at some of the peculiarities of SIC 30; but for the moment it is necessary to accept simply that its presence in the data obscures the positive relationship between the two variables.

When data for SIC 30 were excluded, correlation of ECIs and eight-firm concentration ratios at the two-digit industry level gave the results shown in Table 3-4. Notice that the results show not only a more definite association between the three-year ECI and the industry concentration ratio than the previous correlation results show, but also a higher positive value and a better level of statistical significance for the co-efficient of the average ECI. Consider too that both the value and statistical significance of the coefficients for the five-year and seven-year ECIs progressively deteriorate; this is a pattern that recurs time and again in the results that will be examined later.

TABLE 3-4

Pearson Coefficients of Correlation of ECIs with Adjusted Eight-Firm Concentration Ratios for Two-Digit Industries, Excluding SIC 30
(N = 11)

3-year ECI	+.56 (.036)
5-year ECI	+.12 (.359)
7-year ECI	+.00 (.494)
Average ECI	+.36 (.135)

A third factor that may have contributed to the weak correlation between the ECIs and the concentration ratios is the averaging out of the ECIs for the three-digit industries within each two-digit industry. While correlation of the ECIs with the industry concentration ratios for three-digit industries *within* two-digit industries circumvented this problem, it created the new problem of small sample sizes.

Correlation of ECIs and eight-firm concentration ratios for industries at the three-digit level within two-digit industries.— Examination of the relationship between entry concentration and industry concentration for the three-digit industries within each of the broad two-digit industrial categories confirms that the two variables are positively associated.[4] The data used in these statistical tests also provide a clue regarding the causes of oligopolistic reaction. Within each two-digit industry, entry concentration has tended to be the most intense in those three-digit industries in which selling activities have been paramount for competitive success. To the extent that one can generalize from data relating to only five industries, a tentative conclusion seems to be that marketing considerations, above all else, have prompted firms to counter their rivals' foreign direct investments. In light of what has been said about product-pioneering enterprises, such a conclusion should not come as a surprise. What is the evidence?

The data given in Table 3-5 for SIC 20 (Food and Kindred Products) are illustrative of the kinds of data needed for the correlation results reported in the next several pages. Simple correlation of the average ECIs and the eight-firm concentration ratios gave a Pearson coefficient of $+.70$, statistically significant at the .05 level.

Note the industries with the highest ECIs. The firms in SICs 2031–2035 sell such products as canned foods and condiments. These industries are the domain of such internationally marketing-oriented firms as H. J. Heinz. In SIC 2052 (Biscuits, Crackers, and Cookies) such firms as National Biscuit and General Mills have been in the forefront of international expansion. And in SICs 2022–2034 in which firms sell such items as processed cheese products and evaporated milk, companies like Carnation and Pet have been active foreign investors. All of these firms excel at marketing consumer products, and all have brand names which are internationally exploitable.

The data for the three-digit industries within SIC 20 suggest that when these companies and others like them see a rival investing abroad, a move which may jeopardize an existing or a potential consumer franchise, they are especially prone to move themselves.

---

[4] Data limitations restricted such correlations to five industries.

TABLE 3-5

Data for Correlation of Average ECIs and Eight-Firm Concentration Ratios for Three-Digit Industries Within SIC 20

SIC Code	Average ECI	Adjusted Eight-Firm Concentration Ratio
201	.515	29.3%
2022–2024	.678	50.5
2031–2035	.745	49.0
204	.615	49.0
2052	.695	68.0
207	.667	46.3
208	.600	46.4
209*	.659	56.3

* Because of the small sample sizes, the ECIs for three-digit industries with SIC codes ending in nine were incorporated in the correlations reported on in this section.

In the case of SIC 28 (Chemicals and Allied Products) correlation of the ECIs and concentration ratios for seven three-digit industries gave the results in Table 3-6. Here again we see that entry concentration, at least as measured by the three-year ECIs, is highly positively associated with industry concentration. Also, the underlying data, the values of the ECIs for the individual three-digit industries, tend to corroborate the view that the intensity of oligopolistic reaction is strongly influenced by marketing considerations. Among the seven three-digit industries included in this test, SIC 284 (Soap, Cleaners, and Toilet Goods) has the highest three-year ECI and SIC 281 (Industrial Chemicals) has a quite low three-year ECI. Certainly U.S. soap and toiletry manufacturers depend more on their marketing skills than do U.S. manufacturers of bulk chemicals. In the soap industry as in the food industry the struggle to insure that no rival gains a marketing edge seems to have provoked the most intense defensive investment.

Consider next the fabricated metal products industry. Table 3-7 shows the correlation of the ECIs and concentration ratios

TABLE 3-6

Pearson Coefficients of Correlation of ECIs with Eight-Firm
Concentration Ratios for Three-Digit Industries
Within SIC 28
(N = 7)

3-year ECI	+.73 (.030)
5-year ECI	+.39 (.191)
7-year ECI	+.04 (.469)
Average ECI	+.44 (.159)

for six three-digit industries within SIC 34. Although this was the first time the correlation coefficients for the five-year and seven-year ECIs were higher than the correlation coefficients for the three-year ECI, because of the small sample size, it is unlikely that this pattern has special significance. It is significant, however, that all the ECIs show a strong positive correlation with the industry concentration ratios, although, it is true, that three of the four coefficients are not statistically significant at the .05 level.

TABLE 3-7

Pearson Coefficients of Correlation of ECIs with Eight-Firm
Concentration Ratios for Three-Digit Industries
Within SIC 34
(N = 6)

3-year ECI	+.55 (.131)
5-year ECI	+.79 (.032)
7-year ECI	+.66 (.077)
Average ECI	+.69 (.066)

For the three-digit industries within SIC 34, it is less easy to make a case that firms countered one another's overseas investments principally to maintain some sort of international balance in selling capabilities. In this group of industries SIC 348 (Miscellaneous Fabricated Wire Products) has the highest ECIs. Surely SIC 348 does not evoke the image of marketing-oriented firms. Yet in the industry with the second highest ECIs, SIC 341 (Metal Cans), large U.S. manufacturers like

American Can and Continental Can have led the way overseas, and these firms have traditionally vied as sophisticated
sellers of packaging materials. And at the other end of the
spectrum, the industry with the lowest ECIs, SIC 344 (Fabricated Structural Metal Products), is not one in which it is
likely that marketing capabilities are the most essential factor
for success.

As regards SIC 34, the evidence is hardly clear-cut. Still, it
does not seem to contradict the general notion being advanced
in these pages.

Turning now to SIC 35 (Machinery Except Electrical) and
SIC 36 (Electrical Equipment and Supplies), we find that the
relationship between entry concentration and industry concentration is not as well defined as in the case of the other industries we have looked at. Moreover, when the ECIs of the
three-digit industries in SICs 35 and 36 were correlated with
the corresponding concentration ratios, the results were negative coefficients or positive coefficients with unacceptable levels of statistical significance.

When, however, data for one three-digit industry were excluded from the data for SIC 35 and SIC 36, with one exception, the new correlation coefficients became positive; and
generally speaking, their statistical significance reached acceptable levels. The correlation results for SIC 35 with and
without the exclusion of the data for SIC 358 are given in
Table 3-8. Note that with SIC 358 excluded from the correlation, the coefficients for the five-year and seven-year ECIs became highly positive and statistically significant at the .05
level. Frankly, no explanation, other than an aberration in the
data, comes to mind for the values associated with the three-
year ECI.

The justification for excluding SIC 358 from the test was
that the eight-firm concentration ratio for the industry could
not be adjusted. The industry concentration ratios of the four-
digit industries within SIC 358 ranged from 72% to 26%, but
so few firms established manufacturing subsidiaries abroad in
SIC 358 that it was not possible to identify which of the four-

TABLE 3-8

Pearson Coefficients of Correlation of ECIs with Eight-Firm
Concentration Ratios for Three-Digit Industries
Within SIC 35

	Including SIC 358 $(N = 7)$	Excluding SIC 358 $(N = 6)$
3-year ECI	−.40 (.184)	−.31 (.276)
5-year ECI	+.49 (.132)	+.77 (.037)
7-year ECI	+.51 (.122)	+.74 (.045)
Average ECI	+.17 (.358)	+.56 (.123)

digit industries should be included in the calculation of the
concentration ratio for SIC 358. Accordingly, a weighted average concentration ratio, based on all the four-digit industries
within SIC 358, may have misrepresented the industrial concentration in SIC 358 if only segments of SIC 358 were involved in international expansion.

Concerning the second issue of interest to us, the influence
of marketing motives on firm interaction, the evidence for SIC
35 roughly parallels that for the industries already examined.
The two three-digit industries with the highest ECIs are SIC
357 (Office and Computing Machines) and SIC 352 (Farm
Machinery). Whereas advanced and rapidly changing technology prevails in SIC 357, only relatively stable technology
prevails in SIC 352. Yet, the leading firms in both industries
heavily stress marketing activities.

Certainly, in the case of SIC 357, IBM has become the
world-wide archetype of the marketing-oriented high technology company. And in the case of SIC 352, the struggle for
farmers' allegiance among such firms as International Harvester, Deere, and Ford has always been in terms of such marketing variables as distribution and customer financing. To be
sure, the essentials for market success are not the same in these
two industries. Yet even casual knowledge of the competitive
practices common in the industries suggests that their member
firms put a premium on their marketing capabilities.

In contrast, the member firms in the two industries with the lowest ECIs, SIC 353 (Construction and Related Machinery) and SIC 355 (Special Industry Machinery), tend to rely heavily on product characteristics and product economies to sell their goods. In part this may be because a high proportion of sales in these industries are to industrial customers. In part it may be that it is especially difficult by marketing means alone to differentiate the products of these industries. Regardless of reasons, these industries are not ones that conjure up the names of a number of firms renowned for their marketing activities.

Finally, let us consider the relationship between entry concentration and industry concentration, and the influence that marketing considerations may have on the relationship, for SIC 36 (Electrical Equipment and Supplies). As was the case with SIC 35, the inclusion of one three-digit industry in the correlations obscures what are otherwise fairly strong positive relationships between the ECIs and industry concentration ratios.

SIC 364 was excluded here for the same reason that SIC 358 was excluded from the previous correlation. Within SIC 364 the industry concentration ratios for the four-digit industries ranged from 96% to 26%. But, for want of sufficient data, it was not possible to calculate a concentration ratio for SIC 364 based only on those four-digit industries engaged in international expansion. Certainly the dramatic improvement in both the value and the statistical significance of the coefficients in Table 3-9, when SIC 364 was not included in the test, suggests that its data are somehow misleading.

With SIC 36, as with the other four industries we have examined, there is reason to believe that the intensity of oligopolistic reaction is heightened when rivals struggle overseas to protect some sort of existing or potential marketing franchise. The two three-digit industries with the highest ECIs are SIC 361 (Electric Test and Distributing Equipment) and SIC 363 (Household Appliances). Although sales success probably hinges more on technical product characteristics than on marketing effort in SIC 361, the reverse is clearly the case in SIC

TABLE 3-9

Pearson Coefficients of Correlation of ECIs with Eight-Firm
Concentration Ratios for Three-Digit Industries
within SIC 36

	Including SIC 364 (N = 8)	Excluding SIC 364 (N = 7)
3-year ECI	−.12 (.386)	+.65 (.058)
5-year ECI	+.09 (.418)	+.63 (.066)
7-year ECI	−.11 (.395)	+.43 (.166)
Average ECI	−.04 (.464)	+.65 (.059)

363. For household appliance manufacturers, marketing is the name of the game. True, as the Italian appliance onslaught in Europe demonstrated, production economies are important too. Nonetheless, the fortunes of appliance manufacturers rest largely on their ability to establish brand preferences and broad distribution systems in the markets they serve.

Contrast the importance of effective marketing to appliance manufacturers with its importance to firms in the two industries in SIC 36 with the lowest ECIs: SIC 362 (Electrical Industrial Apparatus) and SIC 366 (Communications Equipment).[5] Product characteristics and price principally determine sales in SICs 362 and 366. Buyers rely on performance and economic criteria, not necessarily on brand loyalty, when judging between competitive products in these industries. Of course manufacturers do their utmost to sell their products, but still marketing *per se* is not sufficient to get the job done. In SIC 36, therefore, the situation is like that in the five other industries we have looked at.

Within all two-digit industries examined, rival firms seem to have countered one another's direct foreign investments most promptly in those three-digit industries in which the marketing function has been of uppermost importance. In part this tendency may be related to firm behavior that differs between

[5] Note that household radios and TV sets, products requiring substantial sales support, are not included in SIC 366; they are classified in SIC 365.

sellers of consumer goods and sellers of producer goods. Certainly many of the industries with high ECIs fall within the consumer goods category. But the anomalies, e.g., the computer industry with its high ECIs, suggest that the simple consumer-goods producer-goods dichotomy cannot account completely for the observed relationship.

The inadequacy of this one explanation is to be expected, however. Bear in mind the basic findings considered so far in this chapter. In many industries, including a number outside of the five two-digit industries examined in detail, entry concentration has been positively associated with industry concentration. Industry structure has had a pervasive influence on the intensity of reaction among oligopolists regardless of whether or not they have been marketing-oriented enterprises. To be sure, rivals apparently have minimized risks most readily when the risks were perceived as having something to do with their market positions or their marketing capabilities. Still, this observation simply means that marketing-oriented firms have been especially sensitive to industry structure. The total picture, though, is much more complex than this.

III. Industry Leaders and Industry Followers

The relationships between ECIs and four-firm concentration ratios and between ECIs and marginal eight-firm concentration ratios.—One possible shortcoming of the eight-firm concentration ratio necessitated correlating the ECIs with two additional industry concentration ratios. The shortcoming has to do with the symmetry of market shares among many industry rivals. If, for instance, all eight leading firms in an industry controlled roughly the same share of industry shipments, the eight-firm ratio would be a valid guide to that industry's degree of concentration. If, however, the shares of the eight were asymmetrical—say two firms each controlled 30% of shipments and the remaining six together controlled 10%—the eight-firm ratio could be a misleading measure of the effective concentration in the industry. Correlation of the ECIs with the adjusted four-firm concentration ratios and with the adjusted marginal eight-firm concentration ratios provided two cross-checks for the possibility of asymmetry.[6]

In view of the fact that the correlation between the adjusted four-firm concentration ratios and the adjusted eight-firm concentration ratios for 34 three-digit industries (the same three-digit industries used previously) was +.97 (.001), there was little reason to expect that the relationships between the four-firm concentration ratios and the ECIs and the eight-firm concentration ratios and the ECIs would differ appreciably. Correlation of adjusted four-firm concentration and ECIs for industries at the three-digit level of aggregation gave the results shown in Table 3-10.

TABLE 3-10

Pearson Coefficients of Correlation of ECIs with Adjusted Four-Firm Concentration Ratios for Three-Digit Industries
(N = 34)

3-year ECI	+.26 (.071)
5-year ECI	+.41 (.009)
7-year ECI	+.32 (.034)
Average ECI	+.37 (.015)

Though the results in Table 3-10 and those obtained when the ECIs were correlated with the eight-firm concentration ratios are very similar, it is nevertheless not safe to conclude that

---

[6] The marginal eight-firm concentration ratio is the percentage of shipments in an industry supplied by the fifth through eighth firms. Richard A. Miller ("Market Structure and Industrial Performance: Relation of Profit Rates to Concentration, Advertising, and Diversity," *Journal of Industrial Economics*, Vol. XVII, No. 2 [April 1969], pp. 104–118) demonstrates that although the four-firm concentration ratio for 106 U.S. industries (roughly three-digit SIC industries) is positively correlated to several measures of profitability, the marginal eight-firm concentration ratio is negatively related to these measures. Miller's interpretation of this finding is that some form of implicit collusion or monopoly-like behavior may be possible among the leading few members of an oligopoly; but as the number of oligopolists increases, firms in the second rank are inclined to include price competition among their competitive tactics.

the relationship between the level of market dominance and the pattern of entry concentration is the same for the leading four and the leading eight firms of an industry; for when the marginal eight-firm concentration ratios were correlated with the ECIs, the results were as shown in Table 3-11.

TABLE 3-11

Pearson Coefficients of Correlation of ECIs with Marginal Eight-Firm Concentration Ratios for Three-Digit Industries

(N = 34)

3-year ECI	+.10 (.285)
5-year ECI	+.12 (.252)
7-year ECI	−.01 (.485)
Average ECI	+.09 (.312)

Neither the value of these coefficients nor their level of statistical significance gives us reason to believe that, with the exception of the first four leading firms in an industry, there is an association between entry concentration and industry concentration. To be sure, the distinction made here between the first four and second four firms in an industry is artificial to the extent that it is based upon the organization of the data.

Nevertheless, the results reported in Tables 3-10 and 3-11 call attention to an important point. The association we have repeatedly seen in this chapter between the ECIs and the industry concentration ratios is the result of the behavior of a few leading firms in each industry. Unfortunately, there is no way of knowing whether it is the result of the behavior of the leading two, or three, or four firms. Nonetheless, rivalry among the few leading contenders in most industries apparently has been the wellspring of oligopolistic reaction.

But this conclusion cannot be accepted without reservation for a reason that was suggested at the beginning of the chapter in the section called "Qualifying the Hypothesis." The nub of the argument is that when a few leaders produce a very high percentage of an industry's output and, as a consequence, their actions are highly interdependent, the timing and placement of their foreign direct investments may be determined by an understanding (implicit or explicit) among them that excessively intense oligopolistic reaction is contrary to the best interest of all.

Up to a point, of course, leaders in such industries are inclined to match one another's direct investments: no firm simply turns over foreign markets to its rivals. But on the other hand, the diseconomies involved in all member firms' countering immediately one another's moves should dictate a commonly held policy of restrained competitive response. If rivals in highly concentrated industries think along these lines, oligopolistic reaction among them should not be especially intense. In terms of the overall statistical relationship between entry concentration and industry concentration, we should expect that it would be nonlinear in character.

IV. Regression Results

Nonlinear relationships between the ECIs and the industry concentration ratios.—The test for a nonlinear relationship between entry concentration and industry concentration involved regressing the three-year ECIs for 34 three-digit industries on a second-order polynomial equation that included both the eight-firm concentration ratio and the square of this ratio.[7] Bear in mind that the four-firm and eight-firm concentration ratios were highly positively correlated, so that the use

---

[7] Scatter diagrams in which the ECIs were plotted against the concentration ratios did not indicate that the relationship between the variables could be represented by either exponential or logarithmic functions.

In other formulations of the regression equation, a dummy variable was used to distinguish between consumer goods industries and producer goods industries. Although the results of such regressions were of questionable statistical significance—and thus not given—the results did suggest that the positive relationship of the ECIs to industry concentration is stronger for consumer goods industries than for producer goods industries. Thus, the regressions corroborate, though not in a statistically significant way, the argument advanced in Section II of this chapter.

of one or the other as the independent variable would make little difference in the results, which are shown in Table 3-12.

TABLE 3-12

Regression Results: Three-Year ECIs Regressed on Polynomial Function of Eight-Firm Concentration Ratios

Dependent Variable	Intercept	Independent Variables CR_8	$(CR_8)^2$	R^2	F Ratio
3-year ECI	−.44624	+ .03025 (.00708)	− .00024 (.00006)	.39	9.94

NOTE: CR_8 stands for the eight-firm concentration ratio; the standard errors of the regression coefficients are shown in parentheses under the coefficients; and the regression equation was statistically significant at the .01 level.

The negative sign for the squared coefficient means that the function took an inverted U shape; the value of the three-year ECI went up as the eight-firm concentration ratio increased to the 60% to 70% range (the maximum point was 63%) and declined as industry concentration continued to rise beyond this maximum.

In the main, regression of the five-year, seven-year, and average ECIs on the same second-order polynomial gave results that were similar to those obtained when the three-year ECI was used. The estimating equation for the average ECI is shown in Table 3-13. With this equation, the value of the average ECI increased with an increase in the eight-firm concentration ratio until the ratio reached 67% and declined as the eight-firm concentration ratio rose beyond this maximum point.

One explanation of these results that immediately springs to mind is that they are the consequence of a scale effect. If, for example, high industry concentration were linked to large scale, and large-scale industries were reluctant to invest in any other than the largest of foreign markets, the negative relationship between ECIs and industry structure, at very high levels of concentration, could come about. But the negative relation-

TABLE 3-13

Regression Results: Average ECIs Regressed on Polynomial Function of Eight-Firm Concentration Ratios

| Dependent Variable | Intercept | Independent Variables | | R^2 | F Ratio |
		CR_8	$(CR_8)^2$		
Average ECI	$-.00841$	$+ .02016$	$- .00015$	.41	10.6
		(.00495)	(.00004)		

NOTE: CR_8 stands for the eight-firm concentration ratio; the standard errors of the regression coefficients are in parentheses under the coefficients; and the regression equation was statistically significant at the .01 level.

ship would have little or nothing to do with highly interdependent firm behavior in quite concentrated industries.

The whole issue of scale and its relationship to market size is a complicated one requiring analysis, from several points of view, in Chapters 6 and 8. While full consideration of the scale issue must wait until then, it can be stated here that scale factors apparently have not accounted for the regression results. Rerunning the regressions with a scale variable, a measure of relative average plant size in U.S. industry, substituted for the square of the concentration ratio gave the results presented in Table 3-14.

Though the negative signs associated with the scale coefficients do suggest that large scale is related to low ECI values, the results are certainly open to question. The large standard errors for the scale coefficients mean that the signs of coefficients are not statistically significant. Note, too, that the R^2s for these estimating equations are much lower in value than those previously reported. To be sure, the results shown in Table 3-14 do not demonstrate conclusively that scale factors have not had a hand in shaping the pattern of entry concentration, but they do seem to indicate that scale effects have not been so industry-specific as to produce the relationships observed in Tables 3-12 and 3-13.

With scale discarded as the explanatory factor, we are back to some aspect of interdependency as the agent at work here.

TABLE 3-14

Regression Results: ECIs Regressed on the Eight-Firm Concentration Ratio and a Scale Measure
(N = 34)

Dependent Variable	Intercept	Independent Variables		R^2
		CR_8	S	
3-year ECI	+.26914	+ .00354	− .16575	.13
		(.00163)	(.11177)	
Average ECI	+.44433	+ .00322	− .12751	.22
		(.00110)	(.075321)	

NOTE: CR_8 stands for the eight-firm concentration ratio, S stands for the scale measure, which was specified as the reciprocal of the number of plants with 20 or more employees in each three-digit industry times 100. Data for computing this measure were taken from the *1963 Census of Manufactures*.

Eight of the 34 three-digit industries used in the regression analyses had adjusted eight-firm concentration ratios above the 70% level; 70% was regarded as the upper limit of industry concentration positively associated with the ECIs. It would seem that managements of firms in these industries did not feel the need to counter rapidly the foreign direct investments of their rivals in the industry. The findings support the supposition advanced at the beginning of this chapter that oligopolists in highly concentrated industries apparently recognize that a tight pattern of follow-the-leader is contrary to the best interests of all firms in the industry.

But as we shall see in the next chapter, this is not a complete explanation; for along with high concentration, highly oligopolistic industries have another characteristic that affects their competitive behavior.

Summarizing the findings.—There are two points about the data we have just examined that stand out. First, U.S. industries engaged in international expansion during the post-World War II period have tended to bunch together their foreign direct investments, and it appears that this tendency becomes stronger the more oligopolistic in structure the industry. Second, an increase in market power of the leading firms of an industry seems to result in an increase in the intensity of their competitive responses, but only up to a point. Beyond this point, further increases in the market power of industry leaders appears to reduce the intensity of their competitive responses.

Of significance is that these interpretations and the research results on which they are based are consistent with those of a number of studies that have been made in the field of industrial organization. Three such studies, two by Professor Frederic Scherer and one by Professor Joe Bain, illustrate the point.

V. Findings of Others

The stability of investment in oligopolistic industries.—Professor Scherer in his study of the capital investment expenditure within the United States of 75 U.S. manufacturing industries between 1954 and 1963 found that in concentrated industries investment tends to be bunched together.[8] In his attempt to determine whether capital investment expenditures were more stable "in concentrated or in atomistically structured industries, other things being equal," Scherer found that theory offered little guidance. The principal literature on the topic either supported or denied that concentration was conducive to investment stability.

Since Sherer's own research, however, resulted in his finding a positive correlation between deviations from trend in investment and the four-firm concentration ratio, he then tried to determine whether these deviations from trend were of a cyclical or random character. A finding of cyclical instability

---

[8] Frederic M. Scherer, "Market Structure and the Stability of Investment," *American Economic Review*, Vol. XLIX, No. 2 (May 1969).

would suggest that member firms in oligopolies simply expanded or contracted investment expenditures in response to fluctuations in demand, whereas a finding of random instability would suggest that a different set of factors had been at work.

In point of fact Scherer found that the investment patterns in concentrated industries were largely random in character and that the appropriations-to-expenditure lags in concentrated industries were not significantly different from those in atomistic industries. Thus his conclusion was:

> Summing up, we find that investment outlays tend to be more unstable relative to their trend values in concentrated than in atomistically structured industries, *ceteris paribus*. This greater instability appears to be more the result of low decision-making power dispersion than excessive sensitivity to demand stimuli, although the latter effect cannot be ruled out completely.[9]

On the basis of the findings in this chapter, it would seem that Scherer's conclusions about the domestic operations of U.S. industry would be applicable to their international operations as well.

Intensity of industrial innovation and industry concentration. —This next finding of Scherer's, which focuses on the relationship between competitive effort (specifically innovation) and industrial concentration, brings to light the important point that high levels of industry concentration do not necessarily lead to high levels of innovative effort.[10] In testing the hypothesis that innovative activity (measured in terms of the employment of engineers and scientists) increases with an increase in industry concentration, he found a positive relationship be-

---

[9] *Ibid.*, pp. 78–79.

[10] Frederic M. Scherer, "Market Structure and the Employment of Scientists and Engineers," *American Economic Review*, Vol. LVII, No. 3 (June 1967).

tween his variables up to a four-firm concentration ratio in the 50% to 55% range, but no evidence that innovative activity was more intense at higher levels of the four-firm concentration ratio.

The relationship Scherer found took the shape of an inverted U, and his maximum point was at a four-firm concentration ratio in the 50% to 55% range. Recall that the relationship between the ECIs and industry concentration also took the shape of an inverted U, and its maximum point was at an eight-firm concentration ratio of about 70%. Although it is not possible to adjust these two ratios to make them comparable, the similarity in the effect on competitive effort of industry concentration above these levels is obvious.

Industry profitability and industry concentration.—Professor Joe Bain, who used the eight-firm concentration ratio to test the relationship between industry concentration and profit rates in U.S. manufacturing industries for the years 1936–1940, found that the profit rates in industries with eight-firm concentration ratios above 70% were significantly higher than those of industries with concentration ratios below this level. His interpretation of this finding was that tacit collusion was ineffective in industries with eight-firm concentration ratios below the 70% level. Subsequently, in a review of this study, Bain concluded that, in all likelihood, his finding was also applicable to the years after World War II.[11] Bain's finding that firm behavior tends to change, to become less competitive, when the leading eight firms in an industry control over 70% of industry shipments, is a great deal like the findings of this chapter.

---

[11] The original study is Joe S. Bain, "Relation of Profit Rate to Industry Concentration: American Manufacturing, 1936–1940," *Quarterly Journal of Economics*, Vol. LXV, No. 3 (August 1951), pp. 293–324. He has reviewed this study in Bain, *Industrial Organization*, pp. 438–452.

VI. Testing the Critical Findings

We have now seen that the results of a number of statistical tests support the supposition that the clustering of foreign direct investments has been related to oligopolistic behavior. And we have seen that these results are generally consistent with the findings of others. But one important task remains: to see if these statistical determinations could have been caused by random factors. The need for such testing was established in the preceding chapter, but the job was postponed until the end of this chapter in order to leave the matter open until more complete tests were possible. Now it is time to fulfill the obligation.

Creating randomized ECIs.—The first step toward checking the validity of the reported statistical results was the construction of an alternative set of ECI values for all 54 three-digit industries for which actual values had been computed. The alternative values were based upon randomized subsidiary formations generated by a Monte Carlo simulation process. The randomization process was constrained, however, in one important way that had to do with the overall trend of postwar foreign direct investment by U.S. business.

Clearly, U.S. industry did not expand abroad in willy-nilly fashion. Overall, there was a distinct pattern to foreign direct investment. In the two decades after World War II the number of manufacturing subsidiaries established abroad mounted year by year, reaching a peak of about 300 per year in the early 1960s. Disregarding this overall pattern of investments would almost assuredly introduce a serious bias into any test based on comparing randomized with actual ECIs. Consequently, the Monte Carlo simulation was adapted in such a way that it randomly assigned subsidiary formations to any of the 20 years under study (1948–1967) but the number of formations assigned to each year was weighted by a trend factor. Specifically, randomization by year was weighted by the total number, as reported by the Multinational Enterprise Study, of manufacturing subsidiaries established overseas (excluding Canada) each year in the 1948–1967 period.[12]

Incorporating the trend factor into the randomization process resolved one problem but created another. The new problem is this. If, in fact, many foreign direct investments were motivated by oligopolistic reaction, then some part of the mounting trend in investments is explained by such interfirm behavior. That is, the weighted randomized ECIs may reflect some residual, but unidentifiable, influences of oligopolistic reaction. When, therefore, statistical results obtained with the actual ECIs are compared with those obtained with the randomized ECIs, it should come as no surprise if differences are not striking. By analogy, a bag of apples is being compared with a bag of lemons, with an unknown quantity of apples mixed in among the lemons. As will become apparent in a moment, the difficulty mentioned here seems to be a problem only when the actual and randomized data relating to overall clustering of investments are considered.

As for the details of the Monte Carlo simulation, within each three-digit industry and within each country, the number of subsidiaries formed each year was generated by the process described above. For example, suppose seven subsidiaries were actually established in SIC 283 in Italy in the years 1948–1967. The simulation reassigned the seven to different years on the weighted random basis. One thousand simulations per industry were run.[13] That done, new ECIs were created using the same method of computation as that spelled out in Chapter 2. Finally, the average of the 1,000 runs was taken as the randomized ECI for each industry. (See Appendix E for the randomized values.)

Since the simulation procedure involved substantial computer time, and cost, only randomized three-year ECIs were constructed. Still, in view of the large number of simulations, it

---

[12] These data were taken from Vaupel and Curhan, *The Making of Multinational Enterprise*.

[13] Sensitivity testing suggested that shorter runs could still introduce error into the randomization outcomes.

seemed safe to assume that test results pertaining to the three-year ECIs could be extrapolated to the other ECIs.

The clustering of foreign direct investment.—Recall that in Chapter 2 it was demonstrated that 46% of all subsidiary interactions took place within three-year peak clusters. That figure was arrived at by comparing the total number of interactions that went into making up the three-year ECIs with the total number of interactions that took place in all the years under study. The figure was interpreted as evidence of follow-the-leader bunching of foreign direct investments.

The comparable statistic, based on the weighted randomized ECIs, ranged in value from .428 to .467 with the average less than .46 and statistically different from .46 at the .10 level. At first glance, this certainly appears to be meager support for the claim that oligopolistic reaction has influenced the investment behavior of U.S. industry. But the problem of interpreting these results has already been alluded to. The comparison here is between the actual ECIs, which purport to measure oligopolistic reaction, and the randomized ECIs, which, because they are weighted, may be contaminated by oligopolistic reaction. If this were all that could be done to test the statistical findings, then their validity would undoubtedly remain an open question. Fortunately, other tests gave less equivocal results.

The ECIs and industry concentration.—The central findings of this study are those demonstrating that entry concentration has been related to industry concentration in ways consistent with what oligopoly theory would lead us to expect. For instance in Table 3-1 we saw that the ECIs are positively correlated with the adjusted eight-firm concentration ratios.

Exact replication of the correlation reported in Table 3-1 using the randomized ECIs produced no such results. Indeed, almost perfect noncorrelation was the outcome. Moreover, correlation of the difference between the actual and randomized ECI with the industry concentration ratios produced coefficients equal to or slightly higher than the originals. The results of the Spearman correlation illustrate this important point. The coefficient associated with the actual three-year ECIs in Table 3-1 is +.22. The comparable coefficient for the randomized ECIs is +.004. And the coefficient associated with the difference between the actual and randomized ECIs is +.235. Clearly, it is the difference between random events and what the actual ECIs measure that accounts for the observed positive relationships between the actual ECIs and the industry concentration ratios.

Comparison of regression results based on actual ECIs with those based on randomized ECIs gives a similar picture. When the actual three-year ECIs were regressed on the eight-firm concentration ratios and the squares of the ratios, the results were an R^2 of .39 (see Table 3-12). Regression of the randomized three-year ECIs on the same two independent variables gave an R^2 of only .08. And regression of the difference between the actual and randomized three-year ECIs on the same variables gave an R^2 of .36. Again, whatever the actual ECIs measure beyond purely random events is what gives them their explanatory power. All the evidence so far suggests that this extra factor is some manifestation of oligopolistic reaction. More evidence follows that suggests the same.

4

Industry Stability: Another Determinant of Entry Concentration

I. Industry Structure and Industry Stability

This chapter carries the analysis of Chapter 3 one step forward to establish that direct investment abroad by U.S. manufacturing enterprise has been related not only to industry structure but also to industry stability. A second determinant of the level of entry concentration, industry stability, is thus identified. The meaning of industry stability, as it is used in this chapter, is quite specific. It is measured in terms of the number of U.S.-based parent firms that became, within certain specified time periods, new investors in overseas manufacturing industries. Thus we shall be considering the effects of new entrants into overseas industries on each industry's pattern of foreign direct investments.

As will become clear, oligopolistic reaction tended not to be particularly intense in industries that were stable in the post-World War II years. That is, in industries where the member firms became active foreign investors in the years before World War II, they tended not to counter energetically one another's postwar investments unless new U.S.-based rivals appeared on the scene. When, however, there was an onslaught of new industry entrants, oligopolistic reaction seemed to heat up among all U.S.-based rivals in an overseas industry regardless of how long they had been involved in overseas operations.

Once the relationship between industry stability and entry concentration is made clear, the findings pertaining to both industry structure and industry stability will be combined to develop a model of the competitive behavior of firms investing abroad.

First, however, in order to avoid confusion, an elaboration of the notion of industry stability will be helpful.

An example of the industry stability concept.—One specific example, based on the history of the overseas expansion of two U.S. industries, illustrates the issue to be examined in this chapter. Before the end of World War II, five large U.S. corporations established manufacturing subsidiaries abroad in SIC 301 (Tires and Inner Tubes), whereas, up to that time, only one U.S. corporation established manufacturing subsidiaries abroad in SIC 352 (Farm Machinery). In the postwar years, however, only one U.S. company entered for the first time the tire industry overseas whereas nine entered for the first time the farm machinery industry overseas.

It seems reasonable to assume that during the postwar years U.S. tire manufacturers regarded their overseas industry situation, *vis-à-vis* the international operations of one another, as a fairly stable one whereas U.S. farm machinery manufacturers held the opposite opinion about their own overseas industry situation. After all, only one new U.S.-based rival emerged on the international scene in the tire business; nine new rivals appeared on the scene in the farm machinery business. The question is in what ways have differences in the number of new industry entrants affected postwar entry concentration in these two industries or, for that matter, in any of the industries under study?

In point of fact entry concentration, as measured by the ECIs, was a good bit higher in SIC 352 (Farm Machinery) than in SIC 301 (Tires and Inner Tubes). At first glance this finding may seem both obvious and trivial. With nine new

U.S. parent firms expanding abroad, one might well expect to find quite a few subsidiaries established in SIC 352 leading to the observed high entry concentration. But the data reveal that during 1946–1967 U.S. parent companies set up more overseas manufacturing subsidiaries in SIC 301 (55 in total) than they set up in SIC 352 (43 in total). Consequently, the number of subsidiaries established in each industry does not account for the difference between the ECIs for SIC 301 and SIC 352. Other factors must have produced the differences in entry concentration. And this brings us back to the point that industry stability has probably influenced the investment behavior of U.S. firms. Why so?

Industry stability and oligopolistic reaction.—There are several reasons to expect that rival U.S. parent firms tend to counter one another's investments abroad less energetically under stable industry conditions than under unstable industry conditions. Newcomers pose a number of risks to the pre-existing industry members. If nothing else, when a U.S. parent for the first time expands abroad into an industry, it interjects a new note of uncertainty into an already uncertain business environment. Even if the new entrant is a member of an oligopoly at home, its fellow oligopolists cannot be sure how the firm will comport itself overseas.

If, for instance, the established members of an oligopoly transplant to their overseas operations accepted norms of rivalry, e.g., reliance on product differentiation measures rather than on price competition, they cannot be sure that the new entrant will also apply these norms to its overseas operations. In a word, new entrants on the international scene can upset explicit or implicit understandings that have grown up over the years among veteran U.S.-based foreign direct investors.

Another reason why a newcomer may disrupt industry stability is that it is probably a latecomer. In an effort to catch up with its fellow rivals, to carve out its share of international markets, a tardy firm may feel compelled to compete in overseas markets in a much more aggressive fashion than was its habit at home. Accordingly, it represents more than a normal competitive threat to its U.S. rivals already established abroad.

Next, if a new industry entrant lacks knowledge about international operations, its inexperience creates risks for its competitors in overseas markets. For example, several U.S. parent firms, all old hands in international business, may be considering investing in an overseas market. But an inexperienced newcomer, in its haste to establish a foreign foothold, may accede to the requests of the local government on points that the more experienced firms would not give way on. Or a newcomer may violate locally accepted business norms and by its bumptiousness jeopardize future opportunities for other industry members.

Also, consider the implications of a new entrant expanding overseas whose capabilities are other than those traditionally at hand in an industry. Recall from the discussion in Chapter 1 that product-pioneering firms have relied heavily upon their unique technological and organizational capabilities to nurture their foreign operations. Now suppose a newcomer, a U.S. parent company from outside the customary industry, brings to the skirmish for overseas markets a new set of skills and resources. From the viewpoint of the traditional rivals, the advent of the newcomer with its different and hard-to-assess capabilities may spell the end to their pre-existing international balance of competitive advantages. If the newcomer redefines the rules of international competition, all rivals in the industry may have to apply themselves to protecting their foreign stakes with renewed vigor.

Findings and alternative explanations.—The findings about to be examined support the general view just advanced that industry instability has led to active oligopolistic reaction. Unavoidably the analysis that follows is not simple and straightforward, for the central finding in the next section of this chapter seems altogether obvious. Only when two likely explanations for the finding are disproved does it stand on its own merit and take on explanatory power.

The central finding—the evidence follows shortly—is that the higher the number of U.S. parent firms investing abroad in an industry for the first time in the post-World War II years, relative to the total number of parent firms that ever invested abroad in the industry, the higher the industry's ECIs. In short, the more unstable the industry, the greater the tendency for firms to cluster their foreign direct investments together in the industry. The two explanations for this finding that immediately come to mind are that differences among the ECIs of industries simply reflect differences in (1) the number of parent firms investing in each industry or in (2) the number of subsidiaries established in each industry.

It is important to show that neither of these two explanations accounts for variation among the ECIs. If, for instance, the data indicated that the greater the number of parent firms that entered an industry abroad, the higher that industry's ECIs, or the greater the number of subsidiaries established in an industry abroad, the higher that industry's ECIs, then it would not be possible to argue that the ECIs measure the intensity of oligopolistic reaction. Instead of reflecting differences among industries of competitive interaction, variation among the ECIs would simply be due to differences among industries in the number of parent firms or foreign subsidiaries in each.

Accordingly, the next section of this chapter presents the evidence on the relationship of industry stability to entry concentration and simultaneously lays to rest the alternative explanations for variation among the ECIs.

II. ECIs and the Stability of Industry Structure

Variation among ECIs and the competitive situation.—For the analytical purposes of this chapter the competitive situation in any industry is measured in two different ways: (1) by the total number, at various points in time, of rival parent firms with overseas subsidiaries in an industry and (2) by the total number, at various points in time, of new rival parent firms investing overseas in an industry in relation to the number of pre-existing rivals with overseas investments in the industry. Correlation of the first measure, for a number of industries, with the industries' ECIs indicates whether the intensity of oligopolistic reaction is related to the number of rivals in an industry. Correlation of the second measure, for a number of industries, with the industries' ECIs indicates whether the intensity of oligopolistic reaction is related to the stability of the competitive situation in an industry. Let us consider the two statistical tests in turn.

Variation among ECIs and number of industry rivals.—To determine if the ECIs were related to the number of parent firms investing overseas in each industry, a count was made of (a) the number of U.S. parent companies that at some time within the period 1900 through 1967 had established overseas subsidiaries in each of a number of industries and (b) the number of U.S. parent companies that first established one or more overseas subsidiaries in each industry during 1946–1967.

As a second step, these totals (for 33 industries[1]) were corre-

[1] In this and in a number of other tests, the ECIs were correlated with data from Vaupel and Curhan, *The Making of Multinational Enterprise.* Because, however, there was lack of complete equality between the data in Vaupel and Curhan and the data organized for this research, before the correlations were run an adjustment of the ECIs was made. Vaupel and Curhan used 48 categories for classifying all manufacturing industries; 30 of these categories were individual three-digit industries, and 18 were either two-digit industries or combinations of two or more three-digit industries. By aggregating the ECIs for several three-digit industries, it was possible to create 33 ECIs for industries or combinations of industries that were identical to 33 industries in Vaupel and Curhan.

Although the ECIs were based upon the number of subsidiary formations in the years 1948–1967, whereas Vaupel and Curhan reported the number of subsidiary formations in the years 1946–1967, the discrepancy of two years was considered to have little effect upon the validity of the statistical tests, since relatively few subsidiaries were formed during the immediate postwar years and since in most tests the data were used for their relative rather than for their absolute values.

lated with the corresponding ECIs. The results were coefficients that were low in value and not statistically significant, and showed a random pattern of positive and negative signs. The conclusion to be drawn therefore is that the differences among the ECIs, at least with respect to the 33 industries under study, are not explained by differences in the number of parent firms that established subsidiaries abroad in each industry either during the postwar years or during the entire period covered by the Multinational Enterprise Study.

Variation among ECIs and stability of industry structure.— Whereas the absolute number of postwar industry entrants is not related to entry concentration, the number of postwar industry entrants, relative to the number of pre-existing industry members, is related to entry concentration. To demonstrate this, it was necessary to count the number of parent firms of each industry that first established subsidiaries before 1946 and the number that first established subsidiaries during 1946–1967 and to express these totals as a percentage of the total number of parent firms that at any time had established a subsidiary in the industry. These percentages (66 in all or two for each of the 33 industries) were then correlated with the corresponding ECIs; the results are given in Table 4-1.

TABLE 4-1

**Pearson Coefficients of Correlation of ECIs
with Percentages of Parent Systems**
(N = 33)

	% of Parent Systems with Subsidiaries Pre-1946	% of Parent Systems First Establishing Subsidiaries 1946–1967
3-year ECI	−.20 (.132)	+.18 (.161)
5-year ECI	+.09 (.300)	−.09 (.301)
7-year ECI	−.36 (.020)	+.33 (.029)
Average ECI	−.20 (.134)	+.18 (.160)

Though the level of statistical significance for most of the coefficients is unacceptable, and the five-year coefficient appears to reflect some aberration in the data, a trend of sorts becomes evident when the coefficients are considered in sequence; their values become larger and their statistical significance improves as the time period associated with the ECIs is extended.

A simple model.—The correlation results shown in Table 4-1 suggest that when new entrants break down equilibrium conditions in an industry, the consequence tends to be an outburst of defensive investments. A simple example clarifies this point:

Industry of Manufacturing Subsidiary	No. of Parent Firms with Subsidiaries Pre-1946	No. of Parent Firms First Establishing Subsidiaries 1946–1967	No. of Parents in Industry 1967
SIC AAA	4	5	9
SIC BBB	2	4	6

On the basis of the first correlation results discussed in this chapter, we can say that although there are, at any point in time, more parent firms in SIC AAA than in BBB, AAA will not, for this reason alone, have the higher ECI. In fact, in view of the results shown in Table 4-1, AAA will have the lower ECI. This is so because only about one-half of all AAA's parent firms entered the industry during 1946–1967 whereas two-thirds of BBB's parent firms entered the industry during 1946–1967. From the standpoint of the old oligopolists, those in SIC BBB faced a somewhat more unstable situation than did those in SIC AAA since they had to contend with a higher proportionate onslaught of new rivals.

The inference drawn here, that oligopolists appear more sensitive to proportionate changes than to absolute changes in the number of their rivals, is of course only a common-sense one. A simple modification of the example above will underscore the point. Suppose the same number of new postwar rivals entered AAA as entered BBB. Suppose further that the new rivals represented, say, 40% of all competing firms in AAA and 70% of all competing firms in BBB. Even though the number of new rivals was the same for both industries, it seems perfectly reasonable to expect that the old oligopolists in BBB would feel a greater sense of industry disequilibrium than the old oligopolists in AAA. More active defensive investment in SIC BBB than in SIC AAA is a logical consequence.

Answering an objection.—Some pages back the reader was forewarned that the findings in this section might appear subject to several explanations. One possibility is that variation among the ECIs, rather than having anything to do with industry stability, might be related to the number of parent firms competing in each industry. We have seen that this is not the case. The second possibility is that variation among the ECI's might be related to the number of subsidiaries established in each industry. Consider how the results shown in Table 4-1 raise this possibility.

The data indicate that the greater the proportion of parent firms entering an industry before 1946, the lower the industry's ECIs in the years after 1946. But, it could be argued, this is obvious, for when a high proportion of an industry's parent firms expanded abroad in the prewar years, they probably established most of their subsidiaries in that period. The low postwar ECIs, so the argument could go, are erroneous since they are not based on the relevant prewar data.

Fortunately, the possibility of this sort of bias in the data can be rejected with one easy test. The 33 industries under study were ranked on the basis of the percentage of the total number of parents in each industry that established subsidiaries before 1946, and this ranking was correlated with a ranking of the 33 on the basis of the number of subsidiaries that were formed in each industry after 1946. The result, a Spearman r of .000 (.498), indicates no systematic bias. Veteran U.S. investors apparently set up about as many subsidiaries postwar as did the latecomers to international business.

We have already seen, at the beginning of this chapter, one specific example of this fact. Recall the history of foreign investment in SICs 301 and 352. All but one of six parent companies started investing overseas in SIC 301 in the years before World War II whereas only one of ten parent companies started investing overseas in SIC 352 in the prewar years. Yet in the postwar years more new subsidiaries were established abroad in SIC 301 than in SIC 352. Nonetheless, entry concentration was more intense in SIC 352 than in SIC 301. Clearly, the difference between the number of subsidiaries in each industry does not explain the difference between the industries' ECIs.

If, therefore, differences in the number of subsidiaries do not account for variation among the ECIs, the inference is that the degree of oligopoly stability accounts for the variance. Apparently, when the international structure of an industry became reasonably well-defined before the war and its structure was little disrupted after the war (i.e., relatively few new U.S.-based industry entrants challenged the established industry leaders), parent firms of that industry did not interact intensively after the war. SIC 30 is the most pronounced example of oligopoly stability, which may explain why it recurs as something of an anomaly throughout this study.

Industry stability and industry concentration.—The findings of this chapter fit neatly with those on seller concentration discussed in Chapter 3. There we saw that the higher an industry's eight-firm concentration ratio, at least up to the 70% level, the higher that industry's ECIs. And we saw that above the 70% level the higher an industry's eight-firm concentration ratio, the lower its ECIs. Now these findings on seller concentration are linked to those that relate to oligopoly stability.

For the 33 industries under study in this chapter, those in which a high percentage of all their parent firms expanded abroad before the war had eight-firm concentration ratios at or above the 70% level. There were only two exceptions to this. Thus industries with eight-firm concentration ratios above 70% exhibit two characteristics that account for their tendency toward low levels of oligopolistic reaction: high concentration ratios and structures that were well-established before the war and little disrupted postwar.

With the relationships of industry structure and industry stability to entry concentration identified and interrelated, it is now possible to speculate on the nature of the firm behavior that brought about these relationships.

III. Oligopolistic Reaction: Cooperation or Rivalry?

Variation between ECIs and the number of parent firms in an industry.—The analysis so far has shown that differences in entry concentration among industries abroad are not related to the absolute number of U.S. parent systems that have set up foreign subsidiaries in these industries. That finding, however, was determined in part by the method used for counting parent firms. When therefore the method is altered and the time period under study is restricted to the postwar years, it can be shown that there is an association between the ECIs of an industry and the number of its parent firms, and it can also be shown that this association supports the assumption that rivalry among firms in an industry has resulted in their undertaking defensive foreign investments.

Recall that correlation analysis showed no relationship between the ECIs of an industry and the total number of parent firms that established manufacturing subsidiaries in the industry. This finding, however, is open to criticism if some of the parent firms that expanded into an industry abroad set up their subsidiaries before or after the time spans, i.e., three, five, or seven years, that were used for computing the ECIs; for in this event these parents would have no effect upon the numerators of the ECIs.

We can look upon such parent firms of an industry as anomalies since they did not establish their subsidiaries during the years in which most parent firms in the industry established subsidiaries; and this means that the number of parent firms that entered an industry postwar need not be the same as the number of parent firms whose subsidiaries figured into the computation of an industry's ECIs.

In order to determine the association, by industry, between the number of parent firms and the intensity of entry concentration when firms that were anomalous were excluded from the data, it was necessary to run three correlations. When, for 38 industries,[2] the number of parent firms with subsidiaries regarded as interacting subsidiaries were correlated with the corresponding three-year ECIs, the result was a Pearson correlation cofficient of $-.11$ $(.263)$. When, however, the correlations were run using the five-year and seven-year ECIs, the results were Pearson coefficients of $-.27$ $(.053)$ and $-.32$ $(.032)$ respectively.

These results indicate, in a general way, that as the number of parent companies with interacting subsidiaries in an industry goes up, there is a tendency, though a weak one, for the intensity of entry concentration in that industry to decrease. Before interpreting this finding, it is necessary that we consider how different behavioral patterns of oligopolistic firms may affect the patterns of interaction.

Collusive or noncollusive behavior?—For analytical purposes we can think of oligopolistic firm behavior as if it tended toward one or the other of two extremes. In some industries, under some circumstances firms will tend toward highly cooperative behavior, leading in the extreme to explicit collusion. But in other industries, under other circumstances, firms will tend toward rivalry leading, in the extreme, to destructive warfare. Whereas the first extreme is well within the limits of possibility, it would seem unlikely that many oligopolists under study would carry rivalry to the point of destroying one another.

---

[2] Since the organization of the data for these correlations and those that preceded was somewhat different, it was possible to expand the coverage from 33 to 38 industries.

Consider first the kind of behavior categorized at the highly cooperative end of the spectrum of conduct. If one argues that collusive behavior is a determinative factor in the international expansion of some industries, then it is reasonable to argue further that the aim of such behavior is foreign market allocation or market sharing among the parent systems operating in these markets. Risk-minimizing defensive investment need not take place; it is replaced by organized and orderly entry into foreign markets. Whatever the means for slicing the pie, the result will be that only one or two parent systems will operate in each foreign market. Consequently, the level of interaction in such markets will be low.

Just as plausible, perhaps, is the argument that colluding firms tend to spread apart their direct investments in a given country, and the result therefore will be an observable pattern of deliberate spacing of subsidiaries. If this is the case, then the seven-year ECIs for these industries will show a closer relationship to the number of parent systems than, say, the three-year ECIs.

But regardless of which of the two arguments is the more reasonable, collusive behavior, nonetheless, will lead to a positive relationship between the number of U.S. parent firms in an industry abroad and the ECIs for that industry. For if the parents of an industry have parcelled out the world as they see fit or coordinated the timing of their direct investments, so that few interactions have taken place, the result will be low ECIs for that industry. Conversely, if the number of parent firms of an industry increases, so that effective collusion becomes more and more difficult, we can expect the ECIs for that industry to increase.

Now consider firm conduct near the other end of the spectrum where behavior, though not exactly warfare of the kind that results in the deaths of industrial rivals, is active and overt rivalry. Firms engaged in this kind of rivalry may be members of oligopolies that are tightly or loosely structured or that lie somewhere in between.

If members of a tightly structured oligopoly—so the argument goes—rival firms will assiduously monitor one another's moves and counter those that may give the initiator a strong leg up. But the more loosely structured the oligopoly, the less urgent is the need for countering one another's moves, since, by definition, the looser the oligopoly the less the interdependence among the member firms. It follows that if rivalry has been the dominant type of behavior, we should find an inverse relationship between the number of parent firms in an industry and that industry's ECIs. This is so because the fewer the rival firms, the greater their interdependence and the greater the penalty for failing to minimize the risks inherent in competitors' moves.

Interpreting the findings.—With the distinction between collusive and noncollusive firm behavior in mind, it is now possible to interpret the correlation results reported on page 96. They suggest that noncollusive behavior, not collusive behavior, has been dominant among U.S. firms engaged in international expansion.

Recall that the correlations revealed negative relationships between the number of parent systems in an industry and that industry's five-year and seven-year ECIs. And also recall that the coefficients of correlation of parent systems in an industry with the industry's seven-year ECI have a greater negative value and a better statistical significance than the coefficients of correlation associated with the three-year and five-year ECIs. Thus the pattern of coefficients, like the values of the coefficients, is inconsistent with the notion that collusive behavior among firms in the industries under study has played a more important role than rivalry in the direct investment process.

Nevertheless, the preceding statement must be qualified to an extent. Some industries that were included in the correlations showed a high degree of seller concentration and oligopoly stability, and they had ECIs that indicated a low level of interaction among the member firms. Hence we cannot say that all industries under study tended toward noncollusive behavior. But we can say that rivalry has been dominant. If, therefore, in most industries collusion has not been an acceptable way, or alternatively an available way, to preserve the international balance of firm capabilities among rival oligopolists, then, of necessity, firms have turned to defensive foreign investment to achieve this end.

Summarizing the findings.—The findings dealing with industry structure (Chapter 3) and those reported in this chapter can be combined and summarized graphically in the form of a curve like the one shown in Figure 4-1.

FIGURE 4-1
Relationship Between ECIs and Seller Concentration

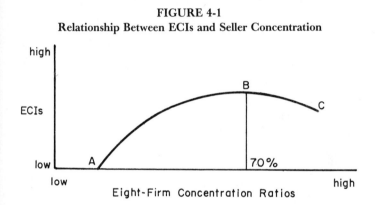

When noncollusive behavior among parents firms of an industry abroad has been the determinative factor, the association between the number of an industry's parent systems and that industry's ECIs is shown by segment AB of the curve in Figure 4-1. When some type of collusive behavior has been the determinative factor, that association is shown by segment BC of the curve. The change in the direction of the curve at point B reflects both the regression results reported in Chapter 3 and the correlation results reported in this chapter.

It is obvious, of course, that the shift in firm behavior has not been as clear-cut or as specific as that implied by the curve. Nevertheless, the findings pertaining to both structure and stability support the conclusion that within a range of industry conditions firms typically tried to minimize risks by matching the foreign investments of rivals with investments of their own. When, however, in a few industries high seller concentration bred a keen sense of interdependency, and when, as a second condition, this commonality of interests was little disturbed by an influx of new industry entrants, member firms had little need to adopt the strategy of defensive investment.

5

Product Diversification

and Entry Concentration

I. Product Diversification and Its Effects on Firm Behavior

At this juncture it is necessary to broaden the scope of analysis beyond consideration of the effects of industry structure on the pattern of foreign direct investments. So far the relationship between product diversification and entry concentration has been ignored. But product diversification is a typical characteristic of the member firms in a number of the product-pioneering industries. And there are reasons for believing that the extent of a firm's product diversity should affect its foreign investment behavior. Accordingly, the links between product diversity and firm behavior need to be identified so that the overall effects of these relationships on how firms invested abroad can be traced out.

Diversification: an alternative to oligopolistic reaction.—
Briefly stated, the argument of this chapter runs along these lines. While the evidence reviewed up to this point is convincing that U.S. firms made their foreign investment decisions with an eye on their rivals, the large enterprises that have expanded abroad have not been mere slaves to the competitive circumstances in any single industry. To the contrary, the majority of these firms built up their stakes overseas by selling a range of products. Consequently, they did not define their competitive situation in terms of only one or two industries.

Rather, because they were diversified, they could opt to penetrate foreign markets with any of a number of products. And
for the same reason they could respond to the foreign investment moves of fellow oligopolists with ventures of their own to
make and sell any of a number of products.

In a word, diversification at home opened up both the aggressive and the defensive foreign investment alternatives for
U.S. parent companies. It follows that when firms had many
options, they could escape to some degree from the necessity of
checkmating every move by rivals. And the more diversified
the firm, the less imperative was it for the firm to make a series
of like-for-like responses. Indeed, for highly diversified firms,
their foreign investment decisions may seldom, if ever, have
been predicated upon reacting to a rival. Instead, they could
set their own course when moving abroad.

What is being postulated here is that the diversified firms
have taken something akin to a portfolio view of their investment opportunities around the world. But note the special nature of this portfolio view. In all likelihood it had nothing to do
with choosing among alternative foreign investments simply
on the basis of anticipated performance at the subsidiary level.
Rather, the diversified firms, like all multinational companies,
probably looked at system-wide returns when making such decisions. And they decided when and where to put their plants
abroad strictly by comparing the expected returns from investment in alternative product lines.

Also, it is possible that managements of diversified firms
have thought in portfolio terms about how they should respond to the moves of rivals. If, for instance, a U.S. company
invested in country A in a particular industry, its diversified
competitor may have believed that it was making a sufficient
response by investing in country A in another industry so long
as both industries had roughly the same sales growth, profitability, and risk characteristics. Matching expected returns
from country A, not matching sales or profits from any one
product, would be the aim of the diversified company.

Now, to the extent that diversified firms have dealt with the world as a portfolio of investment opportunities, their foreign investment decisions should have had little to do with perpetuating oligopolistic equilibria. With many product-market options they were not compelled to follow the risk-minimizing matching strategy set forth in Chapter 1.

Indeed, by spreading their foreign investments over a number of different products, diversified firms were adopting an alternative risk-minimizing strategy. In any case they could either ignore altogether the moves of other U.S.-based firms or, on their own volition, respond with similar moves themselves. It follows that in terms of the basic measure used in this study, entry concentration should be negatively related to product diversification.

So much for the argument in brief. It rests on two key points, and these need to be elaborated if the argument is to hang together. First, it is necessary to establish that product-pioneering firms have tended to diversify their product lines. And second, it is necessary to pursue further the reasons for believing that product diversification has been a determinant of foreign investment behavior. The next two sub-sections take up these tasks.

Diversification and the product-pioneering industries.—Data from one of the landmark studies of diversification of United States industry confirm that product-pioneering firms have usually been product-diversifying firms. Gort's study of the diversification history of 111 large manufacturing enterprises, when his findings are rearranged to fit the purposes of this study, reveals the following situation as of 1954. Of the surveyed firms, those whose primary activity fell in any one of the 12 international two-digit industries (i.e., the product-pioneering industries) manufactured domestically in an average of 18 four-digit industries. In contrast, those whose primary activity fell outside the product-pioneering industries manufactured in an average of 7 four-digit industries.[1] Recall that the industries in this second group were those excluded from analysis (Chapter 2) since overseas investment in them was practically nil.

Moreover, the tendency for the member firms in some industries to diversify has persisted for many years. Gort noted that the highly diversified firms of the 1920s, by the standards of that time, were, in most cases, the highly diversified firms of the 1950s, by 1950's standards. Thus member firms in product-pioneering industries have long had a penchant for diversification.

Gort's observations on the motives for product diversification bear upon the issue at hand. Not surprisingly, Gort found that companies tended to diversify into high-growth industries. But he found an even more important stimulus for diversification: firms were strongly attracted into industries with high rates of technological change. He concluded that diversification into such industries was self-reinforcing. Firms with specialized managerial or technical skills could diversify into the high-technology industries. Having diversified one step, companies further built up their capabilities for managing innovation. They then had an advantage over other firms for taking the next diversification step.

Gort's conclusions should strike a familiar note. He observed that firms with specialized managerial and technical skills spearheaded diversification at home. We have seen (Chapter 1) that firms with similar skills led the way in foreign expansion. Apparently diversification experience in the United States equipped many of the product pioneers with the technical and organizational expertise to broaden their stakes overseas.

Data from the Multinational Enterprise Study indicate that product-pioneering firms have, in fact, carried their special penchant for diversification into their overseas operations. As

---

[1] These data are adapted from Michael Gort, *Diversification and Integration in American Industry* (Princeton: Princeton University Press, 1962), pp. 38–39.

of 1966 companies whose primary foreign manufacturing activity fell in any of the 12 international two-digit industries had, on the average, operations in six overseas three-digit industries. In contrast, those whose primary activity fell outside these 12 industries manufactured overseas—in a very few subsidiaries—in an average of only three three-digit industries. Moreover, on the average, each of the firms in the product-pioneering industries manufactured abroad in three to four three-digit industries outside its primary two-digit industry. The comparable figure for firms not in product-pioneering industries was two three-digit industries.

Now even though the preceding few paragraphs demonstrate a connection between product pioneering and product diversification, they should not be interpreted as indicating that the level of diversity for the typical firm in each product-pioneering industry has been uniformly high. As we shall see shortly, the average level of diversity of the firms in each of these industries has not been identical. The question arises therefore how variation in the level of the average diversity by industry influenced the foreign investment behavior of each industry's member firms. The approach used in the next several pages to raise up some possible answers to this question is to contrast the principal characteristics of diversified firms with those of narrow product-line firms.

The diversified firm.—A number of studies have been directed at determining why U.S. industry diversifies. Gort's *Diversification and Integration in American Industry* has been mentioned already. Chandler's *Strategy and Structure* is another that immediately comes to mind.[2] But since this inquiry has been extended to the international sphere only recently, the present analysis must rely primarily on ideas that are the outgrowth of studies of diversification at home. Note, however, that the evidence collected so far indicates that generalizations about di-

---

[2] A. D. Chandler, Jr., *Strategy and Structure* (Cambridge: The M.I.T. Press, 1962).

versification in the United States are, in the main, applicable to diversification at the international level.[3]

It appears that management has turned to diversification with any one, or a combination, of three general goals in mind. It has pursued diversification in order to accelerate enterprise growth, to obtain above-normal levels of enterprise profits, or to spread the risks touching the enterprise. To attain any or all of these aims management of the diversified firm has adopted a distinctive operating philosophy. Its principal characteristic is the rule that the firm shall have no overriding commitment to any one product line. In conformity with this precept, management is inclined to judge each of the firm's product lines according to its relative profitability and demands upon the resources of the firm.

Successful implementation of this diversification strategy depends upon the firm's capabilities to operate in multiple product-market sectors. Accordingly, the diversified firm attempts to amass the human talents and to build the organizational competencies which will enable it to exploit new products it generates itself or gains through acquisitions. Thus the basic strength of the diversified firm stems out of the same body of acquired expertise that has impelled growth among the product pioneers.

Regarding the first goal of the diversified firm, growth, it appears that in general it has been successful in attaining it. Gort, as already noted, observed that firms diversified into high-growth industries. More recent studies have shown that well-diversified firms enjoy especially high growth rates.[4] For the firm accustomed to growth, one can assume that its expansion reinforces management's desire to see the firm become larger still.

This raises an important point pertaining to foreign invest-

[3] John M. Stopford, "Growth and Organizational Change in the Multinational Firm" (unpublished doctoral dissertation, Harvard Business School, 1968).

[4] See, for example, Richard J. Arnould, *Diversification and Profitability Among Large Food Processing Firms*, U.S. Department of Agriculture Economic Report No. 171 (Washington: Government Printing Office, 1970). In this study the author reviews many of the principal findings on the economic performance of the diversified firm.

ment decisions by the diversified firm. For if the preceding assumption is more or less correct, then it is reasonable to assume
further that when management of the diversified firm is faced
with decisions of allocating the firm's resources to one of two
alternatives—to the protection of a market where the firm and
several of its strong rivals are all competing for market growth
or to the development of a new, perhaps untested market
where the growth opportunity appears especially attractive—
it will tend to opt for the second alternative.

Next, as to profitability, it is an easy matter to find substantial evidence that well-diversified firms have not been more
successful than less-diversified firms at earning high rates of return.[5] One may argue here that the measures of return commonly used by researchers are inadequate if managements operate according to perceptions of return not captured by
simple financial ratios. But in view of the lack of convincing
evidence to the contrary, it seems safe to conclude that diversification is no guaranteed route to high profitability.

What the evidence unequivocally shows, however, is that diversified firms are able to reduce the variability in their total
profitability.[6] Diversification thus appears to be a kind of insurance by which any one risk is minimized as a result of a
firm's operating in multiple fields of uncertainty. Hence the
notion, already advanced, that diversification can serve as an
alternative to risk-minimizing checkmating seems to have
some basis in fact.

Here again is an important clue about how the diversified
firm may respond to a rival's establishment of a foreign subsidiary. If it should counter with a subsidiary of its own in order
to protect a proven market opportunity, and, in particular, if
it should adopt such a policy on a global scale, matching direct investment with direct investment, product with product,
and country with country all over the world, this would not be
in keeping with its typical policy of spreading risk.

Of course it would hardly be expected that any diversified

[5] *Ibid.*
[6] *Ibid.*

firm would casually accept the loss of a market to a rival. But if the preservation of a market franchise should call for a sizable financial commitment, it could be expected that the diversified firm, which is not especially committed to one product line and carefully judges the profitability of each, would in no way be compelled to make a direct response unless the figures would more than justify it.

The narrow product-line firm.—In the main, the basic strength of the narrow product-line firm appears to lie with one or a combination of several of four fields of expertise: (1) logistical skills—the ability to extract and transport raw materials or to manage in some other manner the acquisition and utilization of large amounts of natural resources, (2) production skills—the ability to direct one or more relatively complex production processes or to link together several processes that are applicable to a family of products, (3) research and development skills—the ability to manage intensive R&D efforts for a field, such as the biological sciences, where problems are highly interrelated, and (4) marketing skills—the ability to direct sophisticated or intensive marketing programs for a limited range of products.

Typically, these skills are product specific. Of course this specificity is in part the result of history. Firms that over many years attend solely to the manufacture and sale of a limited range of products naturally circumscribe their capabilities. And in part this specificity is determined by the need to master skills in depth and to employ resources *en masse* in order to produce and market successfully certain types of products.

Regardless of the cause, it is characteristic of management of the narrow product-line firm to possess a high level of competence that is product specific and, we can suppose, to realize that its skills are not readily transferable to other product lines. It can be assumed therefore that it will take whatever steps necessary to protect an established market if that market is threatened by a rival and will do so with the belief that it can win the battle or at least hold its own.

Moreover, since such firms focus their energies on the marketing of a narrow range of products, they accumulate a secondary set of selling skills that are specific to each market. But the transfer of their marketing skills and marketing manpower from one foreign country to another may not be an easy matter. Thus when a specific market is threatened, the firm must react promptly and decisively or run the risk of losing its investment in skills and manpower specific to that market.

We know, for example, that in the early years of expansion abroad by U.S. business many firms established small selling organizations in foreign markets they exported to and that over the years both their export sales and selling organizations increased in like proportions. When therefore the postwar investment scramble got under way, which brought to many foreign markets new competitors from the United States, the narrow product-line firms with well-established marketing organizations were often faced with the problem of how to protect their investments. The establishment of local subsidiaries represented one answer.

For many narrow product-line companies where vertical integration is pronounced,[7] profits can depend to a large extent upon earnings from the beginning stages of production; and in such cases it is often crucial that the firm control its sales outlets in order to guarantee itself profits. Moreover, since many such firms are prepared to operate at very low profit levels at the distribution stage (the petroleum industry is a case in point) these narrow product-line firms have more than sufficient reasons for countering the foreign direct investments of rivals. The alternative is loss of system-wide profits through the loss of market access.

---

[7] There is a sharp negative correlation between product diversity and vertical integration. Simple correlation of one of Gort's measures of product diversity (the average number of four-digit industries per company for firms grouped into 11 two-digit industries) with one of his measures of vertical integration (integration employment as a percentage of total employment for firms grouped into the same 11 two-digit industries) gave a Pearson r of $-.62$ (.021). The data were taken from Gort, *Diversification and Integration in American Industry*, pp. 36 and 81.

Organizational structures.—Since this discussion is concerned with differences between diversified and narrow product-line firms and how such differences may lead to differing responses to competitive threats abroad, one final matter that requires attention is the dissimilarity in their organizational structures. Such a dissimilarity does exist. Stopford has shown that whereas diversified firms tend to be organized around product lines and, if multinational, tend to adopt world-wide product divisions, narrow product-line firms tend to be organized around functions and geographical areas and, if multinational, tend to adopt world-wide functional and area organizations.[8]

Diversified firms with world-wide product divisions emphasize performance by product rather than by geographical area. This emphasis has two implications for defensive investment. First, because each product division is judged almost exclusively on the basis of profit criteria, it is under pressure to allocate its resources to its most profitable opportunities regardless of country. Profit demands force each division to ignore geographical loyalties. Under the system, division managements cannot afford the luxury of making defensive investments merely to maintain the presence of their products in all "promising" markets.

And second, because each division competes for company resources, any single division's defensive investment proposals are likely to be turned down if other divisions can make a better case for the use of company funds or manpower.

In contrast, the typical organizational structure of the international narrow product-line firm may create pressures that result in the firm's making a prompt direct competitive response in markets that appear threatened by an industry rival. For example, in many such firms, one senior executive is responsible for a particular area of the world where the firm operates. Since he is judged on the basis of the sales and profits of his area, quite naturally he will have a vested interest in his

---

[8] Stopford, "Growth and Organizational Change in the Multinational Firm."

particular territory. In the face of a competitive threat in one of his countries, he will argue for a direct defensive response even though company funds might be employed more profitably elsewhere. Stated somewhat differently, area-based organizational structures may breed a parochial point of view, which, because it puts protecting individual country stakes above company-wide considerations, leads to active checkmating of rivals' moves.

At this point, we are now ready to turn to the facts. All the evidence which we shall consider seems to confirm that the chain of reasoning advanced in the last few pages is fairly near the mark.

II. Relationships Between Product Diversification and Entry Concentration

The evidence in summary.—The evidence presented in the next few pages demonstrates that the greater the extent of U.S. parent firms' overseas product diversification, the fewer have been the firms' like-for-like responses to the moves of rivals. Stated in terms of the ECIs, the findings indicate that the ECIs are strongly negatively related to several different measures of product diversification.

Furthermore, when different measures of product diversification are correlated with the ECIs, several important facets of the relationship between the two variables are brought to light. To begin with, on an industry-by-industry basis, product diversity within the United States is apparently unrelated, or only weakly negatively related, to entry concentration overseas. On the other hand, product diversity abroad is highly negatively related to entry concentration abroad.

But additional evidence shows that this last statement needs qualification. When firms diversify from one three-digit industry into another within the two-digit industry that is their primary overseas activity, then diversification is indeed strongly negatively related to entry concentration. When, however, firms diversify into industries outside of their primary overseas two-digit industry, diversification is much less strongly negatively related to entry concentration. Thus far-afield diversification has apparently not been a frequently selected response to competitive threat.

The foregoing points will be elaborated further, but before that can be done, it is first necessary to describe the several quantitative measures of product diversity used to generate the findings.

Product diversity indexes.—Testing for the postulated relationship between diversity and the ECIs called for two measures of product diversity: one a measure of diversification in the United States and the other a measure of diversification overseas. The reason for the two indexes is that in order to make comparisons and to draw some general conclusions it was necessary to classify and ultimately to rank U.S. industries according to the average level of diversity of their member firms, both at home and abroad.

The task of devising measures of diversity involved four simple operations which, for summary purposes, can be described as product counts at the three-digit industry level aggregated to the two-digit level. The basic statistical data for the measures were taken from the *Fortune 1966 Plant and Product Directory* and the Multinational Enterprise Study. The general procedure involved (1) grouping the firms under study on the basis of their primary three-digit industry at home and abroad, (2) counting the total number of three-digit industries that firms grouped together manufactured in at home and abroad, (3) obtaining a simple average of the number of three-digit industries in which these firms operated, and (4) aggregating the data resulting from step 3 to the two-digit level by computing the simple average of the indexes for all three-digit industries within each two-digit industry.

One basic shortcoming of both indexes is immediately obvious. They are based simply on a count of the total number of three-digit industries that firms grouped together manufactured in (see step 2), but all industries that figure into that total are given equal weight. Unfortunately, limitations on sales data specific to diversification abroad precluded using the more reliable type of weighted index to measure diversity overseas. For the sake of comparability, only an unweighted index was used to measure diversification at home. Thus it is important to keep in mind that the indexes used here measure only the breadth of diversification.[9]

Adjusting the overseas diversity index.—Extreme observations complicated the task of devising the index of diversity abroad. Within each three-digit industry one firm typically exhibited a much higher degree of diversification and another a much lower degree of diversification than was usual for firms in the industry. Since in all probability these extreme cases would have distorted the results of the correlations, before the indexes were aggregated to the two-digit level, the index for each three-digit industry was adjusted by excluding from its underlying data the two corporations that exhibited the highest and lowest degrees of product diversity. The adjustment, however, did not substantially alter the indexes: the result of correlation of the adjusted overseas product diversity indexes at the two-digit level with the unadjusted indexes was a Pearson r of +.83 (.001).

Correlation results.—Simple correlations of the ECIs with the indexes of product diversity in the United States and with the unadjusted and adjusted indexes of product diversity abroad gave the results shown in Table 5-1.

Most of the coefficients associated with the adjusted and unadjusted measures of product diversity abroad are significantly and negatively related to the ECIs. The data convincingly make their point. In those overseas industries populated

---

[9] For a review of the theoretical and empirical problems associated with defining and measuring diversification, see Gort, *Diversification and Change in American Industry*, and Arnould, *Diversification and Profitability Among Large Food Processing Firms*.

TABLE 5-1

**Pearson Coefficients of Correlation of ECIs
with Indexes of Product Diversity**
(N = 12)

	Product Diversity within U.S.	Product Diversity Abroad (raw)	Product Diversity Abroad (adjusted)
3-year ECI	−.20 (.267)	−.18 (.283)	−.56 (.029)
5-year ECI	−.12 (.351)	−.37 (.120)	−.52 (.042)
7-year ECI	−.16 (.306)	−.70 (.005)	−.70 (.006)
Average ECI	−.19 (.277)	−.43 (.081)	−.68 (.008)

by firms with only one or two dominant products, the move by one firm to establish a subsidiary frequently prompted like responses from its rivals. In contrast, in industries populated by multiproduct firms this type of investment behavior apparently seldom occurred.

No such positive inferences can be drawn from the coefficients associated with the measure of product diversity within the United States. The link between diversification at home and investment behavior abroad is at best a tenuous one. In part this may be explained by the rather surprisingly low similarity between industries' levels of diversification in the United States and overseas. For the 12 two-digit industries under consideration, the Pearson coefficients of correlation of the United States index with the unadjusted and adjusted overseas indexes were +.32 (.156) and +.35 (.134) respectively.

Diversification at home vs. abroad.—Product diversity by U.S. industry has been much more extensive within the United States than abroad. Table 5-2, with both diversity indexes based on the same sample of firms from the Multinational Enterprise Study, shows how great the difference was as of 1966.

Historical bias undoubtedly figures in the picture presented here. Gort points out that the diversification process within the United States has been under way at a fairly steady pace since

TABLE 5-2

Product Diversity by Two-Digit Industry

Industry	Average Number of Three-Digit Industries Within U.S.	Overseas (unadjusted)
20	8.0	4.8
26	8.8	5.5
28	9.9	5.4
29	7.8	7.8
30	18.8	8.6
32	11.4	6.0
33	9.8	5.6
34	11.4	5.6
35	7.6	6.3
36	17.2	6.3
37	15.6	6.4
38	13.5	6.6

the late 1920s. Yet, diversification abroad by U.S. industry has been limited to more or less the last 20 years.

A second problem further complicates interpreting the figures in Table 5-2. Overseas diversity is measured only in terms of the number of separate products manufactured abroad. Yet multinational enterprises can achieve their objective of diversification in foreign markets through exports. And this can take place well before they engage in direct investment overseas. Later, even after they have set up plants abroad, they can continue to supply part of their product line through exports. Therefore, U.S. industry's product diversity in foreign markets, when exports and locally manufactured goods are considered together, is probably somewhat greater than that indicated in Table 5-2.

Notwithstanding the shortcomings of the data in Table 5-2, it still seems safe to presume that product diversity overseas does not match up to product diversity within the United States. Why is this likely to be the case? Regrettably, studies directed at finding an answer to just such a question have not been especially popular among researchers, so that explanations are not readily at hand. Still, several explanations can be advanced with some confidence.

First, the fact that diversification abroad lags diversification at home is consistent with the product cycle model described in Chapter 1. Recall the empirically validated sequence of events portrayed by the model. Product-pioneering firms developed one after another generation of goods for the U.S. market in response to the special characteristics of U.S. supply and demand. At later dates, when supply and demand assumed similar features in foreign economies, U.S. manufacturers exported and subsequently invested in the beckoning markets. But so long as product-pioneering firms continue to innovate and broaden their product lines in the United States, and so long as there is some differential between U.S. and foreign supply and demand characteristics, the dynamics of the product-cycle process ensure that a diversification gap will remain.

Second, there is some evidence that organizational prerequisites constrain the degree to which U.S. companies diversify overseas. Stopford has shown that U.S. corporations have had to develop new organizational forms and systems for controlling world-wide product diversity before they could manage such undertakings successfully.[10] Accordingly, diversification abroad has had to wait for organizational adaptation.

Other somewhat more speculative explanations for the diversification gap have to do with organizational learning. U.S. managements may commonly test out diversification moves at home before they make the same moves abroad. Even though businesses' reliance on this policy is apparently empirically unverified, the need to offset the high uncertainty of overseas operations makes the policy a sensible one. Managers have much to gain in terms of information by holding off diversification abroad until they assess similar ventures at home.

---

[10] Stopford, "Growth and Organizational Change in the Multinational Firm," has shown that firms have had to alter their international organizations in order to cope with a strategy of global diversification.

Another possibility is that some managers have not felt confident enough about their international business skills, newly acquired in some cases, to consider managing multiple product lines abroad.

Finally, economic obstacles have undoubtedly impeded diversification from time to time. Inadequate overseas capital markets, factor immobilities, and institutional barriers such as reserved markets are examples of such impediments to diversification.

Whatever the cause, up through the middle of the 1960s U.S. industry tended to manufacture a narrower line of products in its foreign plants than it manufactured in its plants at home.

Still, the relationship between product diversity and firm behavior depends on more than just the number of product-market options typically available to firms in each industry. The ease with which firms could take up these options has been important, too.

Diversification outside of primary two-digit industries.—A product diversity index based only on diversification into industries outside of firms' own primary two-digit industries should be a good measure of the extent to which companies have the ability to move beyond their traditional businesses. Certainly, thinking in terms of product pioneers' technological and organizational skills, it has been easier for such firms to diversify into industries in their own primary two-digit SICs than into those outside their primary industries. To some degree, their unique skills have synergistic effects when applied in allied industries; these same skills could have little or no value in alien industries. Realizing this, managements most likely saw far-afield diversification as a rather poor way to protect their stakes abroad. In a general way the evidence bears out this premise.

The job of devising the index, both in unadjusted and in adjusted form, to test this point involved the same procedures previously described, with the one exception that only three-digit industries that were those outside a parent firm's primary overseas two-digit industry figured into the computations.

Correlation of the adjusted index with the ECIs resulted in negative coefficients as shown in Table 5-3, but they were substantially less negative than the coefficients in Table 5-1 and, with the one exception of the seven-year ECI, were statistically not significant.

TABLE 5-3

Coefficients of Correlation of ECIs with Adjusted Product Diversity Index: Diversification into Three-Digit Industries Outside Firm's Primary Two-Digit Industry
(N = 12)

	Pearson r	Spearman r
3-year ECI	−.03 (.463)	−.16 (.309)
5-year ECI	−.14 (.329)	−.29 (.177)
7-year ECI	−.43 (.084)	−.55 (.031)
Average ECI	−.19 (.282)	−.34 (.143)

These data, which indicate that diversification outside of a firm's basic industry is negatively related solely to the seven-year ECIs, suggest that such diversification takes place only over the long haul. There is, of course, nothing very startling about this conclusion. In the first place, diversification is not an overnight process; and the more out of traditional businesses it goes, the more is demanded by way of new skills, new organizations, and even, perhaps, new management, and the more time is required to see the process through to completion. In contrast, diversification within the same two-digit industry may require little more than simple adjustments to existing skills and organizations. It follows that only when competitive interaction is measured over a fairly long time span (i.e., by the seven-year ECIs) is there likely to be any evidence of a negative relationship between diversification into unallied industries and entry concentration.

In the second place, it may take some time for diversified firms to reach the conclusion that the grass is greener in new industries. As was mentioned at the beginning of this chapter, firms frequently diversify to grow faster. If competition in an overseas industry picks up in intensity as a result of the arrival of more rivals, the diversifier may be willing to turn the market over to the new entrants and to move on to a new market where the opportunities for growth appear better. But the decision requires time, and so the longer the time span under consideration, the better the chance there is of seeing the diversified firm switch its allegiance from one industry to another.

Geographical diversity: an alternative explanation for the findings in this chapter.—Suppose that product diversity were highly positively correlated with country diversity. Then the inverse relationships observed between product diversity and the ECIs could be accounted for by diversified firms responding to rivals' moves by setting up subsidiaries in countries where they had not operated before. The interpretations of the findings set forth in the last few pages would be spurious. Fortunately, however, this strawman can be easily disposed of.

The average country diversity (which was measured in terms of the number of countries in which each of the corporations under study, as of 1966, had manufacturing operations) for the firms in the six two-digit industries with the highest product diversity (10.9) was roughly the same as the average country diversity of the six two-digit industries with the lowest product diversity (11.8). And the difference between the two averages was not statistically significant. Country diversity is thus ruled out as an explanatory variable.[11]

The case for product diversity as a determinant of entry concentration still stands. Stated therefore as a general conclusion, this chapter's evidence indicates that the intensity of oli-

---

[11] Although geographical diversity does not appear to be associated with entry concentration, the ease with which an industry's products can be transshipped between countries, which lessens the need to establish subsidiaries wherever a rival does, does appear to be negatively associated—other things being equal—with entry concentration. This issue is examined in Appendix F.

gopolistic reaction is dictated by the number and nature of options open to firms to ignore the moves of near rivals. Of importance, this conclusion is not unrelated to that drawn at the end of Chapter 4. In the following section the link between these conclusions is examined briefly.

III. Diversification and Industry Concentration

Diversifying out of concentrated industries.—A final matter that needs to be considered is the effect of an industry's level of concentration on the tendency of its member firms to diversify into other industries. Here the purpose is to offer an additional argument in support of the thesis proposed in Chapter 4 that much of the time rivalry is the principal force behind the kind of oligopolistic corporate behavior under study; and that diversified firms in particular show a tendency to move out from under the umbrella of impediments to expansion, such as those imposed by industries that have high seller concentration.

Gort, for instance, contends that firms operating in the United States tend to diversify out of more into less concentrated industries.[12] It seems safe to say, based on the following correlation results, that Gort's observation can be extended to include the overseas operations of these firms. Correlation of the adjusted index of product diversity used in Table 5-3 with the eight-firm concentration ratios gave a coefficient of $+.41$ (.096), which indicates that as an industry's concentration increases, so too does corporate diversification abroad outside a firm's primary two-digit industry. Whether those firms diversified into less concentrated industries could not be determined owing to the manner in which the data were organized. A rough and ready guess, however, is that such firms would not have diversified into industries even more highly concentrated than those they were already a part of.

Gort's explanation for his finding, which is applicable to the

---

[12] Gort, *Diversification and Integration in American Industry*, Chapters 7 and 8.

one under consideration here, is that managements of firms in tight oligopolies see their opportunities for rapid growth in sales blocked by the dynamics of interdependency; the more aggressive one firm in the oligopoly is in pushing up its sales, the more aggressive toward matching this goal will be its near rivals. Accordingly, to sidestep this kind of oligopoly trap, managements that look upon growth as necessary for corporate survival will turn to diversification.

Now consider how Gort's point relates to the issue, discussed at the end of Chapter 4, of cooperation versus rivalry. Naturally enterprises would like to have both industry stability and rapid growth. If, under conditions of high seller concentration, firms cooperate, either explicitly or implicitly, they can achieve a fair level of industry stability. But the stability has its price: the sales growth rate for the individual firm is constrained more or less to the growth rate of the industry. It would appear that over the years some of the narrow product-line firms, lacking either the will or the way to diversify, were prepared to pay this price. They kept their foreign direct investments within industry bounds. They opted for stability and, of necessity, cooperated in one way or the other with fellow industry members.

But many firms, those ready to diversify, were unprepared to rely solely on stability and cooperation. When they found their sales growth overseas blocked in one industry, they invested in others. And if Gort's evidence is at all applicable to the overseas operations of diversified firms, they moved into industries where there was less of a chance for spontaneous cooperative behavior. Thus the proliferation of foreign direct investments by the diversified firms lends a bit more support to the hypothesis proposed in Chapter 4: that rivalry has been more characteristic of firms expanding abroad than has been cooperative behavior.

6

Competitive Immunities
and Entry Concentration

The next stage of analysis is consideration of three characteristics—scale, innovational effort, and product differentiation—that may be described as forms of protection for the firm against direct competitive threat. Chapter 1 established the need for dealing with these characteristics. There we saw that these were all traits intrinsic to the product-pioneering industries. And if, in fact, these traits isolated product pioneers one from another, they should have diminished the need for checkmating foreign investment. Accordingly, the general proposition to be explored in this chapter is the following: In those product-pioneering industries where one or more of these three characteristics were especially pronounced, entry concentration should have been, other things being equal, at relatively low levels. Presently, the reasons for anticipating negative relationships between these three factors and entry concentration will be set forth at length. But first a word about the evidence presented in this chapter.

Although the evidence confirms the postulate advanced above, it is important to acknowledge from the outset that the evidence is subject to a number of qualifications. Limitations on available data required the use of approximate measures. Some ambiguity in the results naturally followed. For example, measures of plant scale in the United States proved to be poor surrogates for scale requirements in foreign manufacturing operations. Similarly, measures of innovational effort and product differentiation, which had to be narrowly defined in terms of R&D intensity and advertising intensity and had to be based on U.S. data, demonstrated less than absolutely clear-cut negative relationships with entry concentration. Notwithstanding the data limitations, however, the evidence, taken all together, supports the view that the pattern of U.S. investments abroad has been influenced by the characteristics under study in this chapter.

I. Scale Factors and Entry Concentration

Plant scale and market size.—Let us begin consideration of the association between scale factors and entry concentration by examining the conventional scale market-size argument. The shortcomings of this argument, which will become obvious immediately, raise the possibility that scale requirements do more than simply determine where and when U.S. investors have made overseas commitments. They also apparently affect the propensity of rival firms to react to one another's foreign investment moves.

Typically, analyses of scale and foreign direct investment have been directed at determining the relationship between plant scale and foreign market size because, it is argued, the success or survivability of an overseas investment depends on the opportunities for optimizing scale advantages; and this, in turn, requires that the market in a foreign country be large enough to absorb optimum plant-size output.[1]

Yet this argument fails to take into account or is inconsistent with empirical findings like the following:

1. It does not explain why, in a number of instances, U.S. parent firms have so duplicated one another's direct investments

---

[1] For some evidence on this point plus references to other studies on the topic, see A. E. Scaperlanda and L. J. Mauer, "The Determinants of U.S. Direct Investment in the E.E.C.," *American Economic Review*, Vol. LIX, No. 4, Part I (September 1969).

in small or medium-sized markets that the opportunities have been largely removed for any one subsidiary in an industry to benefit from economies of scale.[2]

2. Nor does it take into account the growing tendency, over the last two decades in particular, of U.S. firms to establish subsidiaries in one market for the purpose of supplying multiple foreign markets; and this means, of course, that a subsidiary's location is not necessarily a clear-cut indication of the size of its market.

3. Also left unexplained is the point made by Professor H. W. De Jong that in a number of countries the market for an industry's product is large enough to absorb the output of a number of optimum-sized plants. Then there is the evidence of Professor Joe Bain that in a number of countries average plant size is well below that required for optimum plant efficiency.[3]

4. Moreover, as Professor Raymond Vernon has pointed out with regard to the multinational firm, the notion of scale economies may be extended to include organizational factors beyond those directly related to production.[4]

There are therefore grounds for supposing that the relationship between the scale of U.S. foreign direct investments and foreign market size has not been a simple linear one. It is the

[2] Sundelson, for one, provides evidence on this point: "Argentina may be a good example of how nationalism and the competitive instincts of manufacturers spoil it for themselves and the country. There are 13 manufacturers now turning out some 70 models of cars and trucks on a total production equal to less than 2% of the U.S. volume." J. Wilner Sundelson, "U.S. Automotive Investments Abroad," in Charles P. Kindleberger (ed.) *The International Corporation* (Cambridge: The M.I.T. Press, 1970), p. 246.

[3] See the testimony of Professor H. W. De Jong reported in U.S. Senate, Subcommittee on Antitrust and Monopoly of the Committee on the Judiciary, *Hearings, Economic Concentration, Part 7*, 90th Cong., 2d Sess., 1968, pp. 3608–3636; and Joe S. Bain, *International Differences in Industrial Structure* (New Haven: Yale University Press, 1966), Chapter 3.

[4] Raymond Vernon, "Organization as a Scale Factor in the Growth of Firms," in J. W. Markham and G. F. Papanek (eds.), *Industrial Organization and Economic Development* (Boston: Houghton Mifflin Company, 1970).

argument of this chapter that oligopolistic reaction partially accounts for this ambiguous relationship. Scale considerations apparently have influenced the willingness of rival firms to follow one another abroad. The effects of scale on the process of competitive interaction help to explain why the pattern of foreign direct investments does not comply neatly with the market-size argument. What are these effects and how have they shaped entry concentration?

Scale factors and competitive response.—Large-scale requirements could discourage defensive foreign direct investment in two different ways. They could function as impediments to competitive response. That is, they could affect the ability of firms to respond. Or, they could increase the riskiness of competitive response. That is, they could affect the willingness of firms to respond. If either, or both, were the case, then the higher the typical scale needs in an industry, the lower ought to be entry concentration in the industry. It will be argued here that whereas large-scale requirements diminish to a minor degree the *ability* of firms to make defensive foreign investments, they diminish to a major extent the *willingness* of firms to make such investments.

This argument will be qualified in one important way. In Chapter 3 we saw that the most intensive oligopolistic reaction took place among the leading few firms in each industry. Therefore, these leading firms, because they are caught up in the game of perpetuating oligopolistic equilibrium, may not respond to scale considerations in the same way as late comers to foreign investment do. Before elaborating on this qualification, however, it is first necessary to set forth the general argument.

As regards the ability of firms to respond to the foreign investments of one another, it will be convenient to tackle the issue in terms of some notions advanced by G. B. Richardson in his book, *Information and Investment.*[5] He argues that under

---

[5] G. B. Richardson, *Information and Investment* (London: Oxford University Press, 1960). See particularly his Chapter 3.

competitive conditions the rate of investment is significantly constrained by entrepreneurial ignorance, the time required for marshaling resources, and entry barriers. To be sure, this is hardly an exhaustive roster of all the factors that could prevent firms from responding rapidly to each other's investments. Still, it is a useful checklist. It should be noted that Richardson does not directly associate these factors with large scale. But if such a link could be demonstrated, then it could be further argued that large-scale firms are less able to counter rivals' moves rapidly than are small-scale firms.

Of the three constraints on investment mentioned by Richardson, at least one, entry barriers, has probably had an effect on defensive investment. In the next section of this chapter it will be demonstrated that entry concentration by industry is negatively related to the level of R&D intensity by industry. Barriers to entry are of course one of the well-recognized consequences of R&D activity. But what has this to do with scale? Investigators have identified a fairly robust positive relationship between R&D-generated entry barriers and large scale.[6] Given the positive links among R&D intensity, entry barriers, and scale, it seems safe to assume that large firms have had to contend with more encumbrances to foreign investment than have small firms. Still, it is not clear how much importance can be assigned to scale effects independent of those related to innovational effort. About the best that can be posited is that in R&D-intensive industries, where large scale also happens to be the normal state of affairs, rivals have frequently had to overcome or circumvent a variety of entry barriers before they could counter one another's foreign investments. Accordingly, prompt competitive interaction has seldom been the case in such industries.

Regarding Richardson's first two constraints on the rapidity of competitive response, it is not at all clear that these have in any way deterred or slowed down large-scale firms from

[6] See Gruber, Mehta, and Vernon, "The R&D Factor in International Investment of United States Industries," pp. 28–29.

making defensive investments. On *a priori* grounds there seem to be no especially convincing arguments that large-scale firms are hindered by entrepreneurial ignorance (or a general lack of information for that matter) to a greater degree than small-scale firms. Indeed, as will become apparent in a moment, the opposite case may be more plausible.

As for the time required for firms to marshal the necessary resources to make a competitive response, it is equally unclear that large-scale firms are at any special disadvantage. Richardson identifies what he calls the "transmission interval," or the time needed by a firm to muster resources, and postulates that the pattern of investments in each industry is dictated in part by its transmission interval. A logical extension from this notion is the obvious one that large-scale firms must mobilize more financial and human assets to make their typical foreign investments than must small-scale firms. And if this were the case, firms in industries where large scale was the rule may simply have not been able to react promptly to competitive threat.

But this argument overlooks several crucial points. First, relative to the total resources they have on hand or can acquire, large-scale firms are probably as well-equipped to assemble the means necessary for foreign investments as small-scale firms. Second, and of greater importance, large-scale requirements need not markedly deter foreign investments if firms can offset the requirements with other advantages. Professor Raymond Vernon, for example, has pointed out that large firms benefit from a set of organizational scale advantages that aid them in identifying and seizing new foreign market opportunities.[7] Consequently, there is no particular reason to argue that firms in large-scale industries are especially incapable of responding to the moves of recognized rivals.

At this point a balancing of the pros and cons discussed in the last several pages is in order. So far we have been consid-

---

[7] Raymond Vernon, "Organization as a Scale Factor in the Growth of Firms," in Markham and Papanek, eds. *op. cit.*

ering how scale could affect the ability of U.S. investors to respond to the moves of rivals with moves of their own. No particularly convincing reason was found for believing that large-scale firms cannot respond as rapidly as small-scale firms to competitive threats in foreign markets. True, because innovational effort, which leads to entry barriers, tends to take place in large-scale industries, rivals in such industries may not be able to counter each other as swiftly as they might desire. But in this case the basic impediments to competitive response are entry barriers, not necessarily scale considerations. Accordingly, if firms checkmate each other less energetically in industries where large scale, not small scale, prevails, then their behavior must be principally related to factors other than their ability to countermove. And this brings us to the relationship of scale to the uncertainty and riskiness of foreign investment.

More often than not, foreign direct investments are made under conditions of high uncertainty. And for those U.S. parent firms strongly tempted by the prospects of important scale economies to put up large plants overseas, this uncertainty can be especially disconcerting. For if U.S. investors want to capture scale advantages, they are obliged to make large and frequently lumpy commitments of both financial and managerial resources. This they must do even though the outcomes from their moves are perhaps only crudely predictable.

Indeed, for several reasons it may be more difficult to calculate the expected results from large-scale foreign investments than from small-scale ones. It is not unreasonable to suppose that the uncertainties pertaining to both demand and supply conditions are somewhat greater for large-scale than for small-scale overseas manufacturing operations.

Consider first the demand side. For the large-scale firm counting on high production volumes to drive down unit costs, its success depends on its ability to induce the market to absorb its substantial output. In turn this calls for a fairly accurate reading of both the size and characteristics of demand.

The risk of a misreading for the large-scale firm can be production well to the left of the minimum on its cost curve. But for the small-scale firm, with its flatter cost curve, the risk of a misreading can be not so great a cost penalty.

Consider, too, the supply side. For the large-scale firm, high output quite obviously depends on fairly substantial factor inputs. Again, success hinges upon the firm's ability to assess fairly accurately the availability and quality of inputs in a country or region where the firm may have little experience. And, as with demand, there is always the chance of misassessment. The result, if it turns out to be factor scarcities, can particularly jeopardize costs in the large-scale firm.

Faced therefore with uncertainties that give rise to substantial risks, oftentimes indivisible ones, it is little wonder that large-scale firms may hesitate before taking each foreign investment plunge.

But large-scale firms may be less inclined to counter rivals' foreign direct investments rapidly than small-scale firms for reasons other than purely economic ones. After all, executives, not corporations, make foreign investment decisions. Personal careers are put on the line. And if executives are personally more risk-averse than their corporations theoretically ought to be, there is reason to believe that firms will not undertake big gambles as readily as they undertake small gambles.

A simple example illustrates the point. Picture the managements of firm A (small-scale) and of firm B (large-scale) contemplating overseas expansion. Firm A with $10 million in assets on hand must invest $1 million to establish a foreign subsidiary; firm B with $100 million in assets on hand must invest $10 million to establish a foreign subsidiary. Assume further that both managements anticipate expected returns on their investments of 10%. Still, they must both face the possibility that the investments could go sour. And even though the losses could run, in proportion to total corporate assets, identical for both companies, the decision makers in B are likely to be somewhat more reluctant to take the gamble than their counterparts in A. At least, if the research conducted on executives' risk aversion curves is to be believed, this should be the case.[8]

To sum up, if the preceding arguments concerning uncertainty and risk are anywhere near the mark, then there is reason to expect that large-scale firms will not undertake defensive investment as readily as will small-scale firms. It follows that scale, measured along various dimensions, should be negatively related to entry concentration.

Qualifying the general argument.—But now consider the effects of scale on entry concentration for firms that are industry leaders and for those that are followers. Since it has been shown (Chapter 3) that the positive relationship between entry concentration and industry concentration is largely the result of the behavior of a few leading firms in each industry, it is on the whole probable that for industry leaders, perpetuating the oligopolistic equilibrium takes precedence over scale considerations.

With regard to industry followers, however, the effects of scale on entry concentration are likely to depend on whether the industry is large or small scale. In the first instance, since each subsidiary represents a large increment to productive capacity, as the number of subsidiaries increases, so too do the chances that the contribution of the newest subsidiary will be that of excess capacity for the industry and a costly but not especially profitable investment for the parent firm.

But in the case of small-scale overseas industries, since the newest subsidiary is not likely to contribute to excess capacity to the same extent as its counterpart in large-scale industries, and most certainly is not as costly, it stands a fair chance of being profitable. Translating what has just been said into ECI language, it is to be expected that there will be little or no re-

---

[8] For a discussion of managerial risk-taking attitudes and references to other literature on the issue, see John S. Hammond III, "Better Decisions with Preference Theory," *Harvard Business Review,* Vol. 49, No. 6 (November–December 1967), pp. 123–141.

lationship between scale and the three-year ECIs, a weak negative relationship between scale and the five-year ECIs, and a fairly pronounced negative relationship between scale and the seven-year ECIs.

II. Scale Factors and Entry Concentration: The Evidence

Measures of scale.—Three alternative measures of scale were used to determine how entry concentration by industry varied with scale. Two of the measures were based upon U.S. industry figures and were calculated from data in the 1963 Census of Manufactures. Specifically, they were (1) average value added per establishment in 1963 for industries classified at the three-digit and two-digit SIC levels and (2) average value of new capital expenditures (1958–1963) for each of the 12 two-digit international industries. Correlation of the two measures for industries at the two-digit level gave a rank order coefficient of +.87 (.001).

The third measure, based upon data specific to U.S.-controlled overseas manufacturing enterprises, was the average 1962 assets per subsidiary for each of the 12 international two-digit industries.[9]

As the analysis proceeds it will become clear that the first two measures do not constitute the "best data," based as they are on U.S. industrial experience.

Also, bear in mind that these are alternative measures of scale. Whereas the first reflects the conventional concept of

---

[9] The data for this measure were calculated from Internal Revenue Service, *Statistics of Income, 1962: Foreign Income and Taxes Reported on Corporation Income Tax Returns* (Washington: Government Printing Office, 1969). Had the data used been based on the assets of relatively few subsidiaries, they would have been subject to a historical bias, since over the years most older subsidiaries would have steadily increased their assets. But such a bias is unlikely in this instance since the data reflect the assets of almost 3,600 foreign subsidiaries and since the evidence does not show that all large-scale industries expanded overseas before small-scale ones.

manufacturing economies of scale, the other two mirror less precise notions of scale. While it is true that measures of capital intensity and average subsidiary assets may capture the size of financial investment typically required in each industry, it is also possible that they capture the lumpiness of investment typical in each industry. Consequently, observed relationships between these two measures and entry concentration probably indicate how investment decisions are influenced by both the magnitude and the divisibility of the resources put at risk.

Correlation results.—Rank order correlations of the ECIs at both the three-digit and two-digit industry level with value added per establishment resulted in Spearman coefficients that, though not statistically significant, nonetheless provided tentative evidence of a negative relationship between the variables.[10]

TABLE 6-1

Spearman Coefficients of Correlation of ECIs at Three-Digit and Two-Digit Industry Level with Average Value Added per Establishment at The Three-Digit and Two-Digit Industry Level

| | Three-Digit Industries | | Two-Digit Industries |
	(N = 54)	(N = 34)[a]	(N = 12)
3-year ECI	−.10 (.237)	+.06 (.377)	+.13 (.348)
5-year ECI	−.09 (.259)	+.01 (.496)	−.33 (.148)
7-year ECI	−.17 (.114)	−.19 (.138)	−.29 (.183)
Average ECI	−.12 (.189)	−.09 (.306)	−.22 (.249)

[a] These are the same 34 industries used in correlations described in Chapter 3.

Rank order correlation of the ECIs at the two-digit level with average new capital expenditures gave results similar to those in Table 6-1.

The evidence in Tables 6-1 and 6-2 hardly settles the issue

---

[10] The Pearson coefficients of correlation are not shown in Table 6-1 because they simply confirm that the absolute values of scale in the United States weakly reflect the absolute values of scale abroad.

TABLE 6-2

Spearman Coefficients of Correlation of ECIs with Average New Capital Expenditures for Twelve Two-Digit Industries
(N = 12)

3-year ECI	+.26 (.208)
5-year ECI	−.29 (.183)
7-year ECI	−.31 (.160)
Average ECI	−.17 (.293)

of scale effects, especially in view of the poor level of statistical significance associated with the coefficients. It is possible that correlations using any index of scale based on data specific to the United States would yield equally poor results. Still, the pattern of coefficients in both tables looks like what has been predicted.

When oligopolistic reaction is measured over the short run, within three years, no reliable relationship between entry concentration and scale is observable. Apparently firms that interact promptly tend to ignore problems of scale. But when oligopolistic reaction is measured over a longer time period, five or seven years, so that the evidence reflects the behavior of both each industry's leaders and each industry's followers, scale's impact on entry concentration is observable. It seems that when industry followers take scale requirements into consideration, they undertake defensive investments reluctantly or not at all.

A historical bias?—At this point in the discussion, one question in particular arises: does the evidence of a weak negative relationship between the measures of scale just employed and the ECIs suggest a historical bias?

Recall (Chapter 4) that the propensity of firms to counter the moves of rivals tended to be low in industries that were stable oligopolies both prewar and postwar, and that the low ECIs for these industries were accounted for by the fact that the majority of their parent companies first established subsidiaries prewar, and hence that their oligopolistic equilibria were little disrupted postwar by the arrival of a large number of newcomers.

But now consider the implications when it is supposed that all industries that were well-established internationally prewar, and hence were stable postwar, were those requiring large-sized plants. If this were the case, then the link observed between entry concentration and plant scale might reflect an association between entry concentration and oligopoly stability.

The evidence, however, does not indicate that this sort of bias has been systematically at work. For although some industries in which plants were typically large became well-established internationally prewar, other large-scale industries did not expand abroad to any appreciable extent until after the war. The facts of the matter were determined in the following way. Three-digit industries were classified as large-scale if the value added per establishment, as reported in the *1963 Census of Manufactures*, was $3 million or more. Despite the fact that the cut-off point was arbitrarily determined, industries so classified would appear to be large scale by any standard. Moreover, the use of a slightly higher or lower cut-off point would not appreciably alter the findings. The three-digit industries classified as large scale were:[11]

SIC Code	SIC Title
206	Sugar
261	Pulp Mills
262	Paper Mills, Except Building Paper
263	Paperboard Mills
281	Industrial Chemicals

---

[11] Only three-digit industries falling within one of the 12 international two-digit industries were included in this count. It should be pointed out, however, that for the eight two-digit industries excluded from this study (see Chapter 2), only two three-digit industries had values above the $3 million cut-off level. This confirms the claim that scale economies have been of special importance to firms in the product-pioneering industries.

SIC Code	SIC Title
282	Plastics Materials & Synthetics
291	Petroleum Refining
301	Tires and Inner Tubes
302	Rubber Footwear
321	Flat Glass
322	Glass & Glassware, Pressed or Blown
324	Cement, Hydraulic
331	Blast Furnace & Basic Steel Products
333	Primary Nonferrous Metals
341	Metal Cans
351	Engines & Turbines
357	Office & Computing Machines
363	Household Appliances
366	Communication Equipment
371	Motor Vehicles and Equipment
372	Aircraft & Parts
374	Railroad Equipment

Next the 22 industries were divided into those that expanded internationally prewar and those that expanded internationally postwar. The division was on the basis of whether more than half of an industry's parent firms that ever operated in the industry moved abroad for the first time before 1946 or in the years 1946–1967. The results were that eight became international prewar and 14 postwar. It hardly needs saying that U.S. industries that expanded abroad to an appreciable extent prewar were by no means all large scale. Likewise, those that went international postwar were not all of modest scale. In fact, in some small-scale industries, notably SIC 202 (Dairy Products), SIC 208 (Beverages), and SIC 284 (Soap, Cleaners, and Toilet Goods), the majority of parent firms expanded overseas in the prewar years. In view of these facts, it seems fair to dismiss the possibility of any historical bias at work here.

Foreign asset commitment.—One more measure of scale remains to be dealt with. Consider the coefficients shown in Table 6-3 which are the result of correlating the ECIs with average assets per foreign manufacturing subsidiary for the 12 international industries.

TABLE 6-3

Spearman Coefficients of Correlation of ECIs
with Average Assets per Foreign Subsidiary
for Twelve Two-Digit Industries
(N = 12)

3-year ECI	−.08 (.398)
5-year ECI	−.28 (.189)
7-year ECI	−.47 (.062)
Average ECI	−.27 (.196)

Though these results are by no means startling, when compared with those in Tables 6-1 and 6-2, they clearly suggest that the higher the overall asset commitment that is needed for making a countermove, the greater the reluctance of all but the leading firms to make such a move. But, as in the case of other scale considerations, the problem of assets required for establishing a subsidiary does not appear to deter the leading four or so firms from oligopolistic reaction.

This last point is given additional support when it is considered from the standpoint of the findings presented in Chapter 3 and those to be presented in Chapter 7. First, recall that the positive relationship observed in Chapter 3 between the ECIs and the level of seller concentration by industry was attributed to the behavior of the four largest firms in each industry. Second, though the proof follows in the next chapter, take it as a fact that there is a positive relationship between firm profitability and prompt interaction. Considered in conjunction, these two findings indicate that the industry leaders, those most actively engaged in checkmating one another, can best afford to play the game.

Accordingly, if greater size and greater financial success are what separate the industry leaders from the others, and if, as the evidence shows, the leaders have a strong propensity to interact, it seems very doubtful whether any one of them would refrain from following in the footsteps of the others for the sole reason that to do so would require a substantial financial commitment.

It is not the same, however, for industry followers, since they are firms that tend to be smaller in size than the industry leaders and somewhat less successful in terms of profitability. It is therefore likely that followers would carefully consider the costs involved in pursuing risk-minimizing defensive investment and might regard the costs as substantial enough to warrant their staying out of the game altogether. In short, since they must carefully consider whether the game is worth the candle, the negative relationship between the five-year and seven-year ECIs and the measure of asset commitment can be explained as reflecting the behavior of firms that typically interact later on. If these firms are to survive, they cannot look upon the magnitude of a financial commitment as a secondary consideration.

Scale and the ability of firms to respond to competitive threat. —Recall the discussion in Section I of this chapter dealing with Richardson's notions of the effects of entrepreneurial ignorance and the transmission interval on the rate of investment. There, largely on *a priori* grounds, the possibility was rejected that either of these factors might especially hinder large-scale firms from reacting to the moves of rivals. Now note that the patterns of coefficients in the preceding correlation results offer empirical support for this rejection.

For if firms in large-scale and small-scale industries were equally ready to counter the moves of rivals, but those in large-scale industries could do so only after a lag of, say, three to five years (the time required to acquire information or to mobilize resources), then the values of the five-year and seven-year ECIs should approximate those of the three-year ECIs. But on the contrary, when the coefficients are considered in sequence, it is clear that they become progressively more negative. In short, defensive foreign investment is not so much a question of the ability of firms to undertake the necessary strides abroad as it is their readiness to protect their overseas interests under conditions of uncertainty and risk. Industry leaders apparently give more priority to their competitive positions than to problems of scale. But for industry followers "to talk sense is to talk quantities" (Alfred North Whitehead).

III. R&D and Entry Concentration

Product-pioneering and innovation.—Product-pioneering firms subsist on innovation. Historically this has been true. Chapter 1 identified the incentives that over the years spurred such firms to concentrate on discovering new products. In recent times, in the years after World War II, their preoccupation with innovation has not abated. Moreover, while they have been innovating at home, they have been investing heavily overseas. On the average, innovational effort in the 12 international two-digit industries, measured in terms of R&D expenditures as a percentage of sales, runs about four times as high as it does in those manufacturing industries excluded from this study.[12]

To be sure, not all of the product-pioneering industries are highly R&D-oriented. By industry, average expenditure of company funds (i.e., federal funds excluded) as a percent of sales runs from a low of around .3% for SIC 20 (Food and Kindred Products) to a high of about 3.8% for SIC 38 (Professional and Scientific Instruments). Still, with the exception of SIC 20, the intensity of R&D activity in the product-pioneering industries surpasses that in all the manufacturing industries relatively inactive in foreign expansion.

---

[12] The data reported here were adapted from National Science Foundation, *Research and Development in Industry, 1967* (Washington: Government Printing Office, 1969). Since on an industry basis, the intensity of R&D activity has varied little over the last decade, generalized statements like those made here are valid.

Given then that the nucleus of United States innovational effort lies in the product-pioneering industries but that the intensity of this effort varies from one industry to the next, the question arises how the differences among the industries influenced entry concentration.

R&D and competitive threat.—Firms that exhibit high levels of R&D effort should be protected to some extent from direct competitive threat. Though the literature supporting this contention is vast, it can be boiled down to two general propositions. Technological innovation either confers competitive immunity by fostering barriers to entry or it permits firms to escape from competitive threats by facilitating diversification. Since these are such familiar arguments, the objective here is not to recapitulate them but simply to tie them to foreign investment decision making.

With regard to barriers to entry, the factors bringing them about should operate in either domestic or foreign markets. It is true, of course, that legally sustained barriers are not available everywhere. In some countries and in some industries U.S. firms either cannot obtain product or process patents or else can obtain them only with difficulty. Yet the patentability of innovational output is only a small part of the picture. Entry into highly R&D-oriented industries is precluded, perhaps most importantly, by the high costs of industrial innovation, by its riskiness, and by the existence of scale economies in research activities. And because these factors should apply world-wide, member firms in high R&D industries should encounter rather few new entrants regardless of where they operate around the globe.

The consequences of entry barriers on the pattern of foreign direct investments are obvious. If, for instance, firm A moves into a new market abroad with a unique product or one well protected by a patent, firm B, a rival of A, will be prevented from hopping on the bandwagon immediately even if it should desire to do so. If it is assumed that R&D intensity and output are positively associated, then by industry the intensity of innovational effort should be negatively related to entry concentration.

Furthermore, this negative relationship should be reinforced by the ability of high R&D firms to diversify. Such firms may not be compelled to match one another's moves, for alternative investment opportunities are open to them. The data underlying this study show that an industry's level of R&D activity is positively correlated to a high degree with its level of domestic product diversification and to a somewhat lesser extent with its level of foreign product diversification.[13] Thus in industries where R&D is second nature, if one firm establishes a new foreign foothold, its rivals may, at least in the short run, ignore the firm's moves owing to their opportunities for exploiting their own inventions through diversifying further still. Defensive investment therefore is an option, not an imperative, in such industries.

"Do I contradict myself?"—The view that entry concentration should be negatively associated with innovational effort may appear to be inconsistent with the earlier finding that entry concentration is positively correlated with industry concentration. The problem posed is this. Since it is well recognized that a high proportion of R&D activity on the part of U.S. industry is restricted to relatively few firms in concentrated industries, the intensity of R&D activity may presumably increase as industry concentration increases, and hence one should expect to find a positive relationship between the degree of entry concentration and the level of R&D effort.

But this argument presupposes that for all industries there is a positive relationship between industry concentration and R&D effort, however defined, when a case to the contrary is well supported by qualitative and quantitative evidence.

---

[13] With regard to the domestic operations of U.S. companies, the link between research effort and product diversification is a well-established one. See, for example, the testimony of Jesse W. Markham quoted in U.S. Senate, Subcommittee on Antitrust and Monopoly of the Committee on the Judiciary, *Hearings, Economic Concentration, Part 3,* 89th Cong., 1st Sess., 1965, p. 1275.

For example, as Richard Stillerman pointed out to a U.S. Senate Subcommittee on Antitrust and Monopoly:

> If monopoly power gives a firm the stability, financial resources, and ability to retain the benefits of its research, then we should find that the more concentrated industries are the most research oriented and technically progressive. . . . Nonetheless, the qualitative evidence, scant though it may be, does raise some questions about the proposition that concentration fosters invention.
>
> In the United States, the most concentrated industries are aircraft propellers, primary aluminum, locomotives and parts, cyclic (coal tar) crudes, flat glass, electric lamps (bulbs), telephone and telegraph equipment, safes and vaults, soap and glycerin, gypsum products, chewing gum, carbon and graphite, reclaimed rubber, primary copper, and steam engines and turbines. Not all of these industries are regarded commonly as pacemakers in technology; some spend little on research. If we rank certain major industry groups from highest to lowest concentration, it is difficult to argue that they retain the same ranking in terms of their interest and accomplishments in research.[14]

In a similar vein is Professor Jesse Markham's contention that while "innovative effort is heavily concentrated in oligopolistic industries," [15] neither in theory nor in practice is innovational effort of a firm "a continuous and increasing function of market power." [16]

Also, recall the finding of Professor Frederic Scherer, referred to earlier, that the level of innovational effort within

---

[14] *Hearings, Part 3*, pp. 1082–1083.

For those who may wonder, Mr. Stillerman is, as Senator Hart pointed out, "The co-author of one of the most basic studies of the history of invention. It was published by Macmillan & Co., Ltd., in 1958, entitled *Sources of Invention*. In this he was joined by David Sawers and John Jewkes, Professor Jewkes, of Oxford." *Supra*, p. 1075.

[15] Jesse W. Markham, "Market Structure, Business Conduct, and Innovation," *American Economic Review*, Vol. LV, No. 2 (May 1965), p. 326.

[16] *Ibid.*, p. 324.

some 56 industry groups (measured in terms of the employ-ment of scientists and engineers) increased up to the point where the four-firm concentration ratios reached 55%, but beyond that point, the relationship between industry concen-tration and innovational activity became ambiguous.[17]

The data developed for this study corroborate, in a rough way, Scherer's finding. Six of the 12 international two-digit in-dustries had four-firm concentration ratios over 55%, above which point, as Scherer demonstrated, the effects of market power on innovation are unclear. And in point of fact, for these six industries correlation of their concentration ratios with their average R&D expenditures as a percentage of sales (1959) produced a negative, though not statistically signifi-cant, coefficient: the Pearson r was $-.40$ (.218). In contrast, correlation between the same two variables for the six indus-tries with concentration ratios below the 55% level produced a positive, though again not statistically significant, coefficient: the Pearson r was $+.56$ (.124).

Since the foregoing evidence demonstrates that the level of R&D activity is not positively associated with industry con-centration for all industries, there is no reason to believe that the corollary, i.e., a positive relationship between R&D and entry concentration, should hold. Indeed, the opposite has been postulated, and it is now time to look at the evidence that bears out the postulate.

Correlation of R&D effort with ECIs.—Correlation of the ECIs with the average per industry of R&D expenditures as a percentage of sales for the 12 international industries gave the results shown in Table 6-4.[18] Note that although the preceding correlation results are based on data for a single year, that year marks the dividing line between the two decades covered

---

[17] Frederic M. Scherer, "Market Structure and the Employment of Scientists and Engineers," *American Economic Review,* Vol. LVII, No. 3 (June 1967), pp. 529–530.

[18] The source for R&D expenditures as a percentage of sales was National Science Foundation, *Funds for Research and Development in Industry, 1959* (Washington: Govern-ment Printing Office, 1963).

TABLE 6-4

Coefficients of Correlation of ECIs with R&D Expenditures as a Percentage of Sales, 1959

	Pearson r	Spearman r
3-year ECI	−.34 (.136)	−.46 (.065)
5-year ECI	−.22 (.241)	−.25 (.196)
7-year ECI	+.08 (.403)	−.17 (.293)
Average ECI	−.23 (.232)	−.41 (.091)

by the study; correlation of the measure employed for R&D effort for 1957 for the 12 industries with comparable data for 1967 gave a Pearson correlation coefficient of +.96 (.001).

Next notice that the Spearman ranking correlation gave better results than the Pearson technique; the former reduced the impact of extreme values of R&D expenditures as a percentage of sales, i.e., those for SIC 20 and SIC 38.

Now notice that the three-year ECI is the most negatively associated with the level of R&D activity. Moreover, when the correlations were run using data for the years 1957 and 1967, the results were the same, i.e., when considered in sequence, the value and statistical significance of the coefficients deteriorated.

Interpreting the results.—Two conclusions can be inferred from the value and the sequence of the coefficients. Either member firms in highly R&D-oriented industries do not undertake defensive investments for the reasons mentioned earlier, or they are forced to time their competitive responses differently from firms in industries where R&D is not so important. Probably both of these explanations are valid. On the one hand, firms with a reservoir of innovations have alternative competitive strategies at their command; they are not compelled to make direct responses. And on the other hand, if one U.S. firm wants to follow a rival abroad, it may take some time for the firm to overcome or circumvent any entry barriers that the rival transplants from the U.S. to the foreign market.

A delayed direct response (see the values of the coefficients associated with the seven-year ECIs) would be the consequence.

It is also important to note what these results do not show. They do not demonstrate that firms in industries highly R&D-oriented established fewer subsidiaries than were established by firms in industries less R&D-oriented. Such a finding would be in conflict with what is commonly observed to be the case. For example, Gruber, Mehta, and Vernon found "that the propensity of U.S. industry to invest abroad, when 'normalized' by the U.S. investment level, is higher in the research-oriented industries than in other industries." [19] Bear in mind that the results reported here pertain to the propensity of U.S. companies to interact with one another, not simply to their propensity to establish foreign subsidiaries.

Testing the results.—As a check on the preceding results, an additional test was run in which the ECIs for the 12 industries under study were correlated with the 1967 R&D expenditures as a percentage of sales for the four firms in each industry with the most extensive R&D programs, and these results were then compared with correlation results based upon data for all firms in each industry engaged in R&D, as shown in Table 6-5.

TABLE 6-5

Pearson Coefficients of Correlation of ECIs with R&D Expenditures as a Percentage of Sales, 1967
(N = 12)

	Four firms with largest R&D programs in each industry	*All firms in each industry*
3-year ECI	−.36 (.125)	−.32 (.154)
5-year ECI	−.34 (.140)	−.30 (.174)
7-year ECI	−.30 (.168)	−.22 (.242)
Average ECI	−.44 (.077)	−.40 (.101)

[19] See Gruber, Mehta, and Vernon, "The R&D Factor in International Trade and International Investment of United States Industries."

Although the difference between the two coefficients for a given ECI is not statistically significant, the fact that the coefficients associated with the four industry leaders are consistently more negative than the coefficients in the second column supports the broad general conclusion that firms highly R&D-oriented do not march abroad in lock-step with industry rivals.

IV. Advertising and Entry Concentration

Advertising's effects on firm performance and market structure: a controversial issue.—Neither theory nor empirical facts gives much guidance on what to expect by way of a relationship between entry concentration and the level of advertising intensity. On·the theoretical level one familiar view is that advertising confers competitive immunity by differentiating products. Tendencies toward high firm profits and industry concentration are presumed to be the consequences of the immunity. But this theoretical outlook stands opposed by what can be called "the Telser view." Professor Telser, a man much in the thick of the controversy over the effects of advertising on firm performance, contends that advertising augments competition rather than diminishes it. For according to Telser:

> In conclusion I wish to remind the reader that the theoretical argument for an inverse relation between advertising intensity and the concentration ratio has attracted far less attention than it deserves. Everyone knows the contention that advertising is a source of monopoly and, therefore, expects a positive association between the two. But intensive advertising is often an instrument of competition as well. The entry of new firms and the offering of new brands is frequently accompanied by high advertising expenditures. Hence advertising can enhance competition. Even if advertising does reduce competition in some cases, it can increase it in others. The net effect reveals itself by the ab-

sence of a dependable relation between the advertising intensity and the concentration ratio.[20]

If the first theoretical argument is more or less correct, then one would expect to find a negative relationship between the ECIs and advertising intensity, for firms heavily committed to product differentiation through advertising would cushion themselves to some extent against the demands of matching the moves of recognized rivals. If Telser's argument is closer to the facts, one would expect to find a positive relationship between the two variables.

Unfortunately, the empirical literature on the relationship of advertising to firm performance in U.S. industry does not tip the scale in favor of one or the other of the arguments. Indeed, this is embattled ground. Empirical evidence runs the gamut from showing practically no association between advertising and measures of firm performance and market structure to showing significant association between the variables.[21] Thus it should come as no surprise that the statistical findings about to be examined are rather inconclusive.

Correlation findings.—Since figures on the level of overseas advertising expenditures by industry are generally unavaila-

---

[20] L. G. Telser, "Another Look at Advertising and Concentration," *Journal of Industrial Economics,* Vol. XVIII, No. 1 (November 1969), p. 94.

[21] For a sampling of conflicting views and empirical evidence on this topic, the reader is referred to the following: Joe S. Bain, *Industrial Organization*; Lester G. Telser, "Advertising and Competition," *Journal of Political Economy* (December 1964); William S. Comanor and Thomas A. Wilson, "Advertising, Market Structure, and Performance," *Review of Economics and Statistics*, Vol. XLIX, No. 4 (November 1967); H. M. Mann, J. A. Henning, and J. W. Meehan, Jr., "Advertising and Concentration: An Empirical Investigation," *Journal of Industrial Economics*, Vol. XVI, No. 1 (November 1967); Richard A. Miller, "Market Structure and Industrial Performance"; William S. Comanor and Thomas A. Wilson, "Theory of the Firm and of Market Structures: Advertising and the Advantages of Size," *American Economic Review*, Vol. XLIV, No. 2 (May 1969); Robert B. Ekelund, Jr. and Charles Maurice, "An Empirical Investigation of Advertising and Concentration: Comment," *Journal of Industrial Economics*, Vol. XVIII, No. 1 (November 1969); H. M. Mann *et al.,* "Testing Hypotheses in Industrial Economics: A Reply," *Journal of Industrial Economics*, Vol. XVIII, No. 1 (November 1969).

ble, a measure of advertising intensity had to be calculated from U.S. data. Correlation of average advertising expenditures as a percentage of sales (1960) for the 12 international two-digit industries with the ECIs gave the results in Table 6-6.[22]

TABLE 6-6

Coefficients of Correlation of ECIs with Advertising Expenditures as a Percentage of Sales (1960) for Twelve Two-Digit Industries

	Pearson r	Spearman r
3-year ECI	−.30 (.172)	−.30 (.170)
5-year ECI	−.33 (.150)	−.32 (.158)
7-year ECI	−.37 (.120)	−.16 (.312)
Average ECI	−.39 (.108)	−.36 (.129)

Similarly, correlation of advertising expenditures as a percentage of sales for 1966 with the ECIs resulted in coefficients that closely approximated those above but showed poorer levels of statistical significance.

A word of caution about interpreting these results. They seem to provide qualified support to the proposition that advertising isolates rivals from one another, thereby lessening the inducement for defensive investment. But the intensity of advertising activity and of innovational activity is positively related. For the 12 international industries, rank correlation of the advertising and R&D measures used in this chapter gives a Spearman r of +.44 (.078). Thus the measure of advertising intensity may function largely as a surrogate for R&D effort in the test reported in Table 6-6.

In view of the conflicting opinions about advertising, the

---

[22] The data for advertising expenditures as a percent of sales for 1960 were computed from Internal Revenue Service, *Corporation Income Tax Returns: With Accounting Periods Ended July, 1960–June, 1961* (Washington: Government Printing Office, 1963). Advertising expenditures as a percentage of sales for 1966 were computed from data provided on individual companies classified at the three-digit SIC level and reported in *News Front* (March 1966), pp. 41–43. The Pearson r between these two measures was +.89 (.001).

data that had to be employed, and the collinearity between advertising and R&D, about the best that can be said concerning the preceding results is that they suggest a tentative relationship that is consistent with the main body of findings in the rest of this chapter.

7

Entry Concentration
and Industry Profitability

Up to this point the analysis has focused entirely on the first
two links of a three-link chain. It has explored the relationships between certain characteristics of the product-pioneering
industries and the defensive investment behavior of the member firms in these industries. Now it is time to add the third
link by looking at the relationship between defensive investment behavior and the performance of these industries' firms.
Specifically, this chapter will examine the tie between entry
concentration and one measure of performance, the profitability by industry of foreign operations.

I. Prompt Defensive Investment and the Level of Indus-
try Profits

There are a number of reasons for supposing that industry
profitability has been positively associated with prompt defensive investment. In a moment we shall consider them. And
later on we shall see that the evidence tends to bear them out.
First, however, it must be pointed out that we are about to
confront a "chicken or the egg" issue. Prompt defensive investment may lead, in a way to be explained, to quite profitable
foreign operations. Alternatively, firms in industries with
above-average profits may be the best equipped to make

prompt defensive investment. In this whole matter causality is an open issue, and the data at hand cannot resolve it. Probably the issue is beyond resolution, for it is likely that the two factors to be considered have functioned both as dependent and as independent variables. For analytical purposcs, therefore, it will be useful to look at the level of industry profits and the level of entry concentration as two sides of the same coin. Let us start by considering the profitability side first.

Member firms in profitable industries can best afford defensive investments.—Quite obviously, firms require human and financial resources to counter the foreign investment moves of rivals. And it seems reasonable to expect that firms in industries where profits at home and abroad generally run high either will have such resources on hand or will have the capability of acquiring them. The abundance of existing or potential resources that attend profitability make it possible for firms to play the defensive investment game energetically in any number of ways. A few examples will suffice since the whole point here is a self-evident one.

Generally speaking, in high-profit industries most member firms will have either excess investible capital or, lacking that, ready access on favorable terms to new debt or equity capital. Capital constraints therefore should seldom preclude making checkmating investments whenever they are indicated. To be sure, cash availability, above all else, determines the capacity of firms to respond to one another. But to the extent that their financial strength is reflected in high cash availabilities, member firms in high profit industries can best afford all the many ancillary outlays that go along with investment abroad in physical facilities. Firms expanding overseas have to invest in the acquisition of information and in corporate communication systems to process the information. They have to develop or attract executives capable of managing their foreign operations. They have to adapt, in major or minor ways, products to foreign consumers' tastes. The list could easily go on. The point is obvious, however. There is a not inconsiderable price tag on foreign investment, and those firms most capable of paying the price are the ones who will be least dissuaded by the costs involved from making defensive investments.

Next, high profits from foreign operations should spur firms all the more to counter the moves of rivals. Suppose one firm learns after a few years that its near rival is making a quite handsome return, by industry standards, on its investment in country A. The firm without the investment in country A may or may not think it can match its rival's profit performance in A with a tardy investment. But let the rival move into country B, and it is a safe bet that the other company will not once again allow its rival to capture for itself all the profits. Thus, once industry rivals have seen or tasted high profits in one or a few foreign markets, they will probably contest one another's investment moves all the more vigorously whenever any rival plants its corporate flag in a new overseas market.

Moreover, in industries where entry concentration has in fact been intense, foreign profits have almost inevitably been good. In the next chapter we shall see that the ECIs, particularly the three-year ECIs, are strongly positively correlated with market growth. Certainly in most cases expanding demand fosters firm profitability. Therefore, defensive investment has been most active in those foreign markets where high potential earnings were almost assured and where, naturally, rivals wanted to guarantee their share of high future earnings.

In short, in industries where profits have typically run high at home and abroad, and the two have generally gone together hand in hand, member firms have had both the capabilities and the stimuli to engage in close-order entry concentration. Consequently, we should expect to find industry profitability positively related to the ECIs. And in particular, we should expect to find profitability strongly positively related to the three-year ECIs since, as we have seen throughout this study, industry leaders have been the most energetic defensive investors.

Perpetuating profitable patterns of oligopolistic behavior.—
Now consider the other side of the coin, the argument that
prompt defensive investment leads to high industry profitability abroad. The chain of reasoning has three steps. First, we
know from Chapter 3 that over a wide range seller concentration is positively correlated with the ECIs, especially with the
three-year ECIs. Second, the empirical evidence of others
strongly supports the conclusion that with regard to U.S. industries high seller concentration is related to high levels of industry profitability.[1] So, third, it is possible that when the leading firms in tight oligopolies, which are noted for their
profitability, follow one another abroad in rapid succession,
the result is that they quickly re-establish abroad market conditions and behavioral patterns akin to those they were used to
at home. Thus, profitable interdependency in the United
States is transplanted, via the mechanism of concentrated
entry, to foreign soils.

But note that the argument presupposes that the U.S. firms
can transplant patterns of rivalry. This raises two questions
about foreign market conditions. When firms in highly concentrated U.S. oligopolies follow the leader in fairly rapid succession, what is the effect on industry profitability when the
overseas industry they expand into is composed of many relatively weak local competitors; and what is the effect on industry profits when the foreign market is composed of local oligopolists?

It can be argued that whatever the pre-existing state of
affairs in the overseas market, the new entrants from the
United States will adopt their old familiar patterns of oligopolistic behavior. In the first place, they can expect that after an
initial period of time most of the traditional members of the
club will be together again as local producers and sellers. In
the second place, because they are corporate extensions of
their product-pioneering parents, they enter the market armed

---

[1] For a recently conducted test of this point and references to a number of earlier
studies on the issue, see Miller, "Market Structure and Industrial Performance."

with their special technological and organizational advantages. Not only can they frequently out-compete local rivals on conventional terms, but also they may introduce entirely new dimensions of competition. Consequently, the pre-existence of a number of local competitors need not present an obstacle in the path of the U.S. oligopolists establishing modes of competition that proved profitable back home.

Next take the case in which the new entrants face a pre-existing local oligopoly. If, as is often true, the leading firm in the local oligopoly has established artificially high prices which serve as an umbrella over its less efficient rivals, the competitive effects of such high prices on the new entrants from the United States depend on how many of them have arrived. If, for example, it is early in the game, so that just one U.S. firm has a local subsidiary, its management may reason that it has sufficient production, marketing, and other skills to engage in a price war with the local leader and eventually to take its place.

But later on, as more members of the U.S. club arrive, any aggressive actions on the part of one member will undoubtedly bring forth retaliation from the others, so that it will become necessary to re-establish the old rules of the game in order to assure high profits for all. This being so, it follows that the U.S. oligopolists have no reason to undermine the prices set by the local leader. Instead, they revert to the old competitive habits and customs that proved profitable at home.

Now, as a final point, note that the argument just advanced is not at odds with the earlier position that high industry profitability makes possible high entry concentration. To the contrary, the two arguments are complementary. Profitable operations in the United States and elsewhere, fostered in part by interdependency, endow oligopolists with the financial and human resources needed to exploit new foreign market opportunities rapidly. The rapid-fire invasion of foreign markets by sets of traditional rivals alerts all to the dangers of overly aggressive competitive tactics. Accordingly, the entrants tend to eschew pure price-output strategies and, because they are product pioneers, tend to stress differentiation and innovation strategies instead. High profits in one after another overseas market follow.

So much for conjecture. Let us look at the facts.

II. The Evidence

The measure of industry profitability.—The basic assumption on which the coming analysis rests is that any association to be found between the ECIs and industry performance, defined as average return on assets, would most likely reveal itself in a correlation between entry concentration abroad and industry profitability abroad. Yet this assumption is open to criticism on at least two counts.

First, the customary profitability by industry of domestic operations or of aggregate world-wide operations undoubtedly influences the readiness of firms in the industry to undertake direct investments abroad. And second, managements in certain industries, in particular those with pronounced vertical integration, may think in terms of overall or world-wide profitability and not in terms of profitability in specific foreign markets or of total foreign operations.

The first criticism will not be challenged, for the complex range of issues it opens up is far beyond the scope of this study. Thus, while it is acknowledged that the willingness of firms to undertake foreign direct investments may depend upon a number of financial factors, e.g., world-wide corporate profitability (however defined), liquidity, and debt structure, and the availability and cost of credit at home and abroad, it is also acknowledged that the job of isolating and testing the influences of the factors on the direct investment process will be left to others.

As to the second criticism, that one has already been dealt with. Data on the two international industries that had exceptionally high degrees of vertical integration—SIC 29 (Petroleum and Coal Products) and SIC 33 (Primary Metal Industries)—were excluded from the basic data on which the measure of profitability was based.

For the purpose of devising a measure of profitability, all U.S.-controlled foreign subsidiaries under study, with the exception of subsidiaries in SIC 29 and SIC 33, were classified on the basis of the two-digit international industry they operated in.

The profitability measure itself, which is in effect each industry's average return on foreign assets, is the ratio of an industry's average 1962 profits to average 1962 assets of foreign corporations controlled by U.S. parent firms.[2]

The use of data covering only 1962 immediately raises the question whether the resulting measures are adequate. In answer to that question, it needs to be pointed out (a) that the data on profits and assets were based upon tax return information for a substantially large number of foreign subsidiaries associated with each two-digit industry, (b) that collectively these subsidiaries were established over a long period of time and in many different foreign countries, and (c) that there is no reason to believe that the data on profits and assets for all or a great many subsidiaries in any one of the ten industries were biased by some factor or circumstance unique to the industry in 1962.

Figures on the number of subsidiaries, by industry, that figured into the IRS's calculations on profits and assets are shown in Table 7-1.

Industry profitability and industry characteristics—The first step in uncovering the statistical association between entry

---

[2] The data for the profitability measure were calculated from Internal Revenue Service, *Statistics of Income, 1962: Foreign Income and Taxes Reported on Corporation Income Tax Returns* and relate to U.S.-controlled foreign corporations and their subsidiaries when their principal activity was manufacturing.

Because of the way in which the IRS reports the earnings of foreign branch operations and of extractive operations, it was not possible to adjust the data for highly integrated industries to make their data comparable to those of the other ten international industries.

TABLE 7-1

U.S.-Controlled Foreign Subsidiaries by Industry

SIC CODE	Industry Title	No. of U.S.-Controlled Subsidiaries
20	Food and Kindred Products	444
26	Paper and Allied Products	118
28	Chemicals and Allied Products	1,035
30	Rubber and Plastics Products	99
32	Stone, Clay, and Glass Products	136
34	Fabricated Metal Products	390
35	Machinery, Except Electrical	563
36	Electrical Equipment and Supplies	307
37	Transportation Equipment	208
38	Instruments and Related Products	259

concentration and industry profitability was to establish whether other variables, e.g., average absolute profits, average sales, average assets of U.S.-controlled foreign operations, and the eight-firm concentration ratio, were tied to or influenced the average return on assets by industry. The purpose of this first step was to determine whether any association shown to exist between entry concentration and the measure of industry profitability used could be the result of an underlying association between the measure of profitability and one or a combination of these other variables.

As one would expect, an industry's average absolute profits on overseas operations were positively correlated with its average absolute sales and assets abroad: the Pearson coefficients of correlation were $+.98$ (.001) for both. Similarly (see Table

TABLE 7-2

Pearson Coefficients of Correlation of U.S. Eight-Firm Concentration Ratios with Overseas Industry Characteristics
(N = 10)

Average Assets by Industry	$+.50$ (.069)
Average Sales by Industry	$+.60$ (.034)
Average Profits by Industry	$+.53$ (.056)

7-2) the U.S. eight-firm concentration ratio for each of the ten industries was positively correlated with the same three variables used in the preceding correlations.

When, however, the four variables were correlated with average return on foreign assets by industry, quite a different picture emerged (see Table 7-3).

In view of the value and level of statistical significance of the coefficients associated with all four variables in Table 7-3, there is little reason to believe that they are related to industry profitability.

TABLE 7-3

Pearson Coefficients of Correlation of Industry Characteristics with Average Return on Foreign Assets
(N = 10)

Average Assets by Industry	+.19 (.300)
Average Sales by Industry	+.26 (.231)
Average Profits by Industry	+.30 (.198)
Eight-Firm Concentration Ratios	+.26 (.232)

Entry concentration and industry profitability.—For a rather startling contrast, consider now the results of correlation of the ECIs with the average return on foreign assets in Table 7-4.

TABLE 7-4

Pearson Coefficients of Correlation of ECIs with Average Return on Foreign Assets
(N = 10)

3-year ECI	+.64 (.022)
5-year ECI	+.44 (.099)
7-year ECI	+.32 (.185)
Average ECI	+.58 (.040)

The preceding coefficients, when examined in conjunction with those in Tables 7-2 and 7-3, suggest, first, that return on foreign assets by industry is more significantly and positively related to the pattern of entry concentration by industry than to any of the four other variables we have looked at and, second, that industry profitability is linked strongly to prompt interaction. Defensive investment and profitable foreign operations seem to go hand in hand, especially so for industry leaders.

III. Relating the Profitability Findings to Prior Evidence

Two conclusions were drawn from the findings in the preceding section. First, the profitability of industries' overseas operations have been positively tied in some way to the level of defensive investment in each industry. Second, quick reaction to the investment moves of rivals has been somewhat more profitable than delayed reaction. Both of these conclusions presume that there is a direct link between defensive investment and industry profitability even though it is not clear whether the level of defensive investment is the dependent or independent variable in the equation with profitability. Yet it is certainly possible that one or several of the other factors considered in the previous chapters of this study, not oligopolistic reaction, accounted for the findings in Table 7-4. Consequently, some analytical loose ends need to be tied up.

The next few pages pick up some of the principal points discussed in earlier chapters to see if any of them could serve as alternative explanations for the industry profitability findings.

The number of rivals in foreign markets.—Perhaps the number of rival foreign subsidiaries typically found in each industry explains variation in industry profitability. It could be argued, for instance, that the fewer the subsidiaries commonly established abroad in each industry, the larger each subsidiary's potential share of the profits in foreign markets and hence the higher the industry's average profit performance. But this argument would be consistent with the evidence in Table 7-4 only if the ECIs were strongly inversely related to the number of subsidiaries established by industry. Yet, from Chapter 4, we know that this is not the case; there is no clear-cut relationship between the number of subsidiaries by industry and the value of the ECIs by industry.

Furthermore, since the ECIs were based upon the pattern of interactions in a number of countries, the positive correlation between entry concentration and industry profitability could not be accounted for by the number of subsidiaries established in a single, or just a few, foreign markets.

In other words, what the evidence indicates is not a relationship between profitability and the absolute number of subsidiaries by industry but the relationship between profitability and the degree of oligopolistic reaction by industry. At least, that seems to be the case so far.

Other alternative explanations.—Individually or collectively, firm and industry differences associated with scale, technology, and barriers to entry may explain the positive association observed between prompt defensive investment and industry profitability. It may be, for instance, that firms in industries noted for high returns on assets tend toward prompt oligopolistic reaction because of their (a) small scale, or (b) special technological advantages providing opportunities for monopoly profits, or (c) success at creating multiple barriers to entry into their industry.

As to industries composed of small-scale firms, it needs repeating that the analysis in Chapter 6 has shown that there is no relationship between measures of scale and the three-year and five-year ECIs; oligopolistic reaction among these firms has been no more or less prompt than it has been among firms in other industries. Moreover, if the findings in Table 7-3 are correct or approximately so, then industry profitability abroad appears unassociated with scale.

Consider next the matter of technological advantage. If firms in industries characterized by innovational leads and resulting opportunities for monopoly profits had responded quickly and directly to competitive threats, then their investment behavior would be associated with high profitability of overseas operations. But recall that the analysis in Chapter 6 showed a negative relationship between the level of an industry's R&D efforts and its ECIs. Firms in the technological vanguard apparently shied away from the checkmating game and instead set an independent course for international expansion. Another fact worth mentioning is that among the ten international industries under study, the five with the highest three-year ECIs and highest returns on foreign assets showed an average level of R&D expenditures, as a percentage of sales, that was slightly lower than the comparable average for the remaining five industries.

If the facts do not support the argument that firms that made rapid responses profited from special technological opportunities, neither do they support the notion that firms in industries with high three-year ECIs had exceptionally high profits because of their success at creating multiple barriers to entry into their industries.

When the ten international industries were divided into two groups—the five with the highest and the five with the lowest three-year ECIs and returns on foreign assets—and a comparison was made of the average *number* of parent systems that expanded abroad in the postwar years into each group, the result was that more parent systems entered the first group than entered the second group. The difference, however, was not statistically significant. Furthermore, a higher *percentage* (though again statistically insignificant) of parent systems, calculated by the method in Chapter 4, entered the five industries with the highest ECIs than entered the remaining five industries. It is a reasonable conclusion therefore that firms in industries characterized by rapid oligopolistic response and relatively high profitability have not been unusually successful at keeping out new entrants.

Noncapitalization of assets: a final alternative explanation.— Perhaps the industry profitability findings are misleading because the return on assets figures for one or more of the ten industries under study are seriously in error. Consider the following chain of reasoning. Commonly, U.S. industry does not capitalize such important activities as R&D and advertising. Even though the benefits firms acquire from these activities often boost corporate profits, the benefits are not recorded on corporate books as either tangible or intangible assets. Consequently, for highly R&D-oriented industries or for highly advertising-oriented industries, conventional calculation of corporate profit measures results in artificially high return on assets figures.

Note, however, that the advantages created by R&D or advertising, assets which are hidden in an accounting sense, may allow for fast reaction to rivals' threats. For example, in a consumer goods industry, one firm may promptly follow a rival into a new foreign market if it, the follower, has a trade name that has become internationally established. And if something like this happened in a number of cases, one could stumble upon the observed but misleading positive relationship between prompt interaction and industry profitability.

The foregoing argument, which is based upon some well-founded misgivings about the validity of conventional measures of corporate profits, undoubtedly identifies a chain of relationships applicable to some of the firms in this study's sample base. But the data at the aggregate industry level will not support the argument. For if it were correct, there ought to be a positive association between the return on assets by industry and the intensity of R&D and advertising activity by industry. In fact, for the ten industries, correlation of the return figures with the sum of the R&D and advertising intensity measures (see Chapter 6) gives a Pearson r of $-.37$ $(.148)$. Of course, this one test does not invalidate the argument, but it shows that the sort of bias suggested by the argument apparently does not affect the industry profitability findings.

Summary.—In the last few pages we have seen that industry characteristics alone cannot account for the positive link between the level of each industry's foreign profits and the degree of entry concentration within the industry. One cannot disregard the interdependent investment behavior of U.S. oligopolists and simply presume that their foreign operations have been profitable because they could exploit abroad unique profit-generating advantages initially acquired in the United States. Further, one cannot argue that some industries were more profitable than others overseas simply because they had more advantages to exploit overseas. The struggle among U.S. industry rivals, intensified in the more concentrated industries, to perpetuate some sort of oligopolistic equilibrium in one after another foreign market has somehow played a part in the whole process. In one foreign industry after the next, the onslaught of several U.S. firms, actively contending among themselves along a number of dimensions of rivalry to guarantee that no one firm got the upper hand, apparently tended to insure that they would achieve market dominance.

This is not to argue that firm and industry characteristics have not been important. Of course the product pioneers enjoyed advantages which, when transplanted to foreign soils, gave them some degree of monopoly power. And of course the urge to capture monopoly or quasi-monopoly profits strongly motivated foreign direct investment. But within the product-pioneering industries, firms did not have a completely free hand to pick when and where they would invest abroad. At least, they did not have a free hand once any one of their leading rivals decided to invest in any particular foreign market.

The argument being put forward here, that each industry's profit performance cannot be divorced from the nature of interdependent behavior within the industry, is given additional support by a comparison of the relationship between the three-year ECIs and industry profitability and the seven-year ECIs and profitability. As the figures in Table 7-4 suggest, the link between entry concentration and industry profitability breaks down as time passes and more and more subsidiaries interact in an industry abroad. That this is so is crucial to the argument. For a significantly positive association between industry profitability and any of the ECIs (i.e., the three-year, five-year, or seven-year ECIs) would suggest that industry characteristics, not the behavior of industry leaders, were responsible for the relationship between entry concentration and profitability. That is to say, if the early entrants and stragglers enjoyed equally high levels of profits, there must be something about each industry that accounts for its especially profitable operations.

Put another way, if the correlation coefficients in Table 7-4 associated with the three-year, five-year, and seven-year ECIs were positive but identical, or nearly so, then differences among industries in overseas profitability would almost assuredly have been entirely due to differences in profit-generating characteristics. But since this is not the case, differences among industries in how firms interact must also influence performance. And if this is so, we cannot rule out the earlier argument that brisk defensive investment tends to perpetrate, from one market to the next, profitable patterns of oligopolistic behavior.

8
Entry Concentration by Country

I. Market Characteristics and Entry Concentration

Thus far we have examined entry concentration industry by industry. Now we will look at the matter country by country in order to understand the effects of market size, market growth, and general market stability on oligopolistic reaction.

A nontraditional objective.—The aim of this chapter, to explain how certain foreign market characteristics influenced the investment behavior of oligopolists, differs from the goal of conventional analysis of the foreign investment issue. Usually, investigators have sought to uncover the relationships between economic aggregates or impediments to trade and the total flow or total stock of U.S. direct investments abroad.[1] Here, in contrast, the purpose is to trace out the relationships between economic aggregates, plus a measure of market stability, and the clustering of U.S. direct investments. This distinction is an important one to keep in mind. If the interpretations of the factors motivating foreign investment reported in this chapter depart from those of other investigators, the divergencies can be accounted for by the two different ways of looking at the foreign investment process.

---

[1] See, for example A. E. Scaperlanda and L. J. Mauer, "The Determinants of U.S. Direct Investment in the E.E.C.," *American Economic Review*, Vol. LIX, No. 4, Part 1 (September 1969), pp. 558–568, and Bela Balassa, "American Direct Investment in the Common Market," *Banca Nazionale del Lavoro Quarterly Review*, No. 77 (June 1966), pp. 121–146.

The general line of argument.—Though three leading market characteristics are to be considered, it will be argued that only two of the three have led to variation in entry concentration. As for the two, it is likely that (1) the growth rate of markets and (2) their general socio-political stability have determined the intensity of oligopolistic reaction. The same, however, has probably not been true for (3) the size of markets. The exclusion of market size from the list of determinants is, perhaps, somewhat surprising. Let us therefore consider it first.

Market size and entry concentration.—According to the conventional market-size argument, investment will take place as soon as a foreign market is large enough to permit the capturing of economies of scale. By and large, tests have substantiated the argument. Scaperlanda and Mauer, for example, in their investigation of the effects of market size, economic growth, and tariff discrimination on U.S. direct investment in the European Economic Community (EEC), found that the size of the market (specified as the total GNP of the EEC) was the only independent variable significantly associated with the annual change in the book value of U.S. direct investments in the EEC.[2]

A somewhat analogous test, based on data from the Multinational Enterprise Study, leads to a similar finding. Correlation of the number of manufacturing subsidiaries established during 1946–1967 in the countries sampled to create the ECIs with a measure of their market size (1958 gross domestic product) gave a Pearson coefficient of $+.72$ (.001). Clearly, where U.S. parent firms established their subsidiaries has been related to market size.

But is there reason to believe that variation in market size

---

[2] Scaperlanda and Mauer, *op. cit.* Note that they did not find economic growth a useful explanatory variable. In Section II of the chapter, economic growth is shown to be a determinant of variation among the ECIs by country. This sort of difference in findings has already been alluded to. Whereas market growth may not be associated with the total flow of U.S. direct investments, it apparently does influence oligopolistic reaction. The reasons why are set forth in the next several pages.

was strongly positively associated with variation in entry concentration? The evidence we examined in Chapter 6 suggests not. There we saw that industry leaders tended to counter one another's foreign direct investments regardless of scale considerations. Of course the first member of an industry to make a direct investment in any particular country probably waited until scale advantages were attainable. But once one firm set foot in the foreign market, its near rivals hastily followed even though it meant that all might have to operate at sub-optimal levels of output. Thus, in their rush to offset their rivals' gains, firms oftentimes ignored the link between market size and scale constraints.

Stated in general terms, it appears that even if market size functions as a threshold for initial foreign investment, subsequent defensive investment will depend on other considerations such as the structural characteristics discussed in the earlier chapters of this study. Accordingly, we should expect to find market size, *per se,* a rather poor indicator of the intensity of oligopolistic reaction.

Market growth, however, is a different matter.

Market growth and entry concentration.—It is only natural that rapidly growing foreign markets should attract U.S. investors interested in expanding their stakes overseas. After all, the gains in output needed to meet rapidly increasing demand offer opportunities for economies of scale. And even though defensive investors may ignore scale considerations at the outset, they want assurance that scale advantages will be possible in the future. Rapid growth gives this assurance. If, therefore, future production economies look as though they will outrun any diseconomies associated with growth, the cost trend for potential investors will be in the right direction. Moreover, as a general rule, price pressures should be minimal in buoyant markets. These fundamental considerations should apply to almost all firms.

But for U.S.-based oligopolists the lure of rapidly growing foreign markets should be especially strong. The nature of rivalry within the United States is one reason for this. If, at home, demand is relatively stagnant, then in concentrated industries each firm can grow—leaving aside diversification—only at the expense of its rivals. Interdependency makes attempting firm expansion at a pace greater than market expansion a costly and perilous course to pursue. And even if domestic demand is growing at rates comparable with those in overseas markets, rivals in concentrated industries know that they will capture only something like their traditional share of new business. Thus, at home, the oligopoly trap limits enterprise expansion and perpetuates the distribution of competitive might among rivals.

Overseas growth markets, however, can be a free-for-all. The early bird U.S. investor has an opportunity to expand sales unimpeded by its usual U.S. rivals. Of more importance, the early investor may capture a large share of the market, a share larger than it has at home. In so doing the firm can shift, albeit perhaps only slightly, the balance of competitive muscle between it and its traditional rivals. Of course local rivals cannot be disregarded. But as we have seen, the product pioneers, with their special technological and organizational capabilities, commonly have some edge over local firms. Hence, for U.S. oligopolistic firms, investment overseas in swelling markets has twin attractions: the chance for expansion at rates above those possible in the United States and the chance for some realignment of industry structures.[3]

Note that market growth, not market size alone, gives rise to these attractions. For U.S. investors know that their fellow oligopolists will not be far behind. And if demand is relatively stagnant in a foreign market, even a large one, it will not be too long before rivals will face the same situation in the foreign country that they face at home. This is not to say that U.S. firms avoid investing in large foreign markets. We have al-

---

[3] Balassa was an early proponent of this point of view. He argued that U.S. oligopolistic firms were especially attracted to the Common Market countries because the economic integration and rapid growth of the six made for fluid market structures. See Balassa, *op. cit.*

ready seen evidence to the contrary. It is to say, though, tha U.S. investors give special attention to rapidly growing mar kets, for such markets offer oligopolists their best chance of im proving their lot relative to their rivals.

But beyond this first point, there is the whole matter of in come elasticities of demand. Over the years, and both at home and abroad, these have probably run better than one for the output of firms in the product-pioneering industries. Conse quently, the product pioneers have always had a special stake in economic growth. Certainly history suggests that this has been so.

Recall that the product pioneers repeatedly introduced new products in the United States to match expanding incomes and the upgrading of consumer needs. Recall, also, that their penetration of foreign markets depended on similar income and consumption shifts. The product strategies of these firms have almost always been linked to rising incomes.

And we know for a fact that in the post-World War II years product pioneers' involvement in the international market place has been significantly influenced by income changes in foreign markets. For instance, much of the postwar United States trade pattern can be explained by foreign income elas- ticities.[4]

It should not be surprising, therefore, that firms that have always focused on satisfying needs generated by increasing in- comes should strive especially hard to establish footholds or to protect pre-existing positions in growth markets. The product pioneers' unique capabilities have been geared to exploiting growth situations. It is little wonder that they would fight to protect their interests in such markets.

Accordingly, if each oligopolist wants to make sure that it is the one to collar the advantages of growth, we should find that checkmating investment takes place most actively under high growth conditions.

---

[4] See H. S. Houthakker and Stephen P. Magee, "Income and Price Elasticities in World Trade," *Review of Economies and Statistics*, Vol. LI, No. 2 (May 1969), pp. 111– 123.

Still, there is probably another condition, general market stability, that needs to be met to induce energetic defensive investment.

Market stability and entry concentration.—For a number of reasons oligopolists may be sensitive to the general stability of a country in which they may make a defensive investment. In the first place, an unstable country can be especially hazardous for members of an oligopoly because the risks faced by one may easily be transmitted, via interdependence, to all members of the oligopoly.[5] For instance, owing to some force directly related to a country's instability, one member of an oligopoly may make a move that the other members are compelled to follow, even though they would regard these moves as contrary to their best interests. Or perhaps the host government, following a not uncommon practice, may extract more and more concessions from all members of an oligopoly by playing one off against the other.

---

[5] The arguments developed in the next few pages are analogous to certain ideas in Oliver Williamson, "A Dynamic Theory of Interfirm Behavior," *Quarterly Journal of Economics*, Vol. LXXIX (November 1965). On the issue of stability, Williamson writes:

"The factor that appears to be mainly responsible for shifting the firms in an oligopoly between cooperative and conflict solutions is the condition of the environment. Thus, although oligopolists can be assumed to be continuously aware of their interdependency relationship and the collective advantages of pursuing a qualified joint profit maximization strategy, adherence to a joint profit maximization agreement may be made difficult during times of adversity by current pressing demands that cause short-run own-goals of one or more of the members to override collective considerations. Assuming that when adversity is experienced by one it is experienced generally, deviation by one member of the coalition is likely to induce defensive responses by others, and the entire relationship tends quickly to deteriorate into one of conflict and active competition."

On this same issue, Williamson also speaks of the observations of others:

"However, March and Simon argue that a deterioration in performance (due to an unfavorable change in the condition of the environment) causes the group to reinterpret the relationship between the membership as being more competitive than cooperative, and conflict is apt to result. Bernard also observes that cooperation is conditional on the capacity of the environment to produce satisfaction, and thus adversity poses a threat to an adherence relationship which had been quite stable under more favorable conditions."

In the second place, in an unsettled country, an oligopolistic market structure may constrain the flexibility of an oligopolistic firm when it needs it most. When operating in such a market, one member of the oligopoly may wish to adopt a policy of changing its mode of operations as conditions in the country change, but may find it is unable to do this because several industry rivals are operating in the country as well. For example, suppose three such rivals have subsidiaries in a country whose government is hostile to high levels of advertising expenditure, and the leader of the three wants to discontinue or reduce its advertising expenditures because it is aware that this will not jeopardize its market position but will comply with the desires of the host government. If, however, its rivals were not subject to much government scrutiny because of their smaller sales volume, then the leading firm would hesitate to make such a move on the grounds that this action would give its rivals an opportunity to increase their market shares.

Third, because instability may predispose some members of an oligopoly to turn to collusion as a way of coping with the problems inherent in an unsettled market situation, it may cause other members, those leery of collusion, to be equally leery of unstable environments.

Fourth, a reasonably stable environment may be required in order that oligopolists may practice subtle, complex modes of restrained competition. It often happens that once a country has attained some threshold level of socio-political stability, or has re-established order after a period of turmoil, like Indonesia, firms in oligopolistic industries simultaneously show an interest in making direct investments in the country. This suggests that oligopolists respond not only to a new market opportunity but to one that offers the prospect of restrained competition.

Last, it may be, as Thomas Schelling suggests, that constrained competition requires a steady flow of information between adversaries and that the acts of each firm serve as signals to its rivals.[6] As a result of an interchange of signals, each firm is able to develop a picture of the cardinal features of its principal adversaries and of the measures they may take to protect their well-being.

Once firms have made this kind of assessment of their rivals, it then is possible for them to reach a tacit understanding that prevents competition from breaking out into mutually destructive warfare. But when the social or political or economic environment in which they operate is unsettled, communication may break down because the acts, beyond the routine ones, that firms take to cope with instability represent "noise" in the communications system; and to be successful, this system depends on the giving and receiving of signals that cannot be misinterpreted. Thus a breakdown in the communication system, if unchecked, may lead to a breakdown of the tacit understanding that constrained competition.

Summing up, oligopolists should not hesitate to counter one another's moves into stable foreign environments, but they should be especially shy of following one another into unstable ones.

II. The ECIs by Country

Testing for the relationships between market characteristics and entry concentration calls for the use of country, not industry, ECIs. Since these are new measures, a brief description of how they are calculated is necessary.

What are the ECIs by country?—Recall that to compute the ECIs by industry it was necessary to identify by three-digit industry the maximum number of manufacturing subsidiaries established in 23 countries (see Chapter 2) within three-year, five-year, and seven-year periods and then to sum these interactions by industry across the 23 countries.

---

[6] Thomas C. Schelling, *The Strategy of Conflict* (New York: Oxford University Press, 1963).

When, however, what matters is the pattern of interactions in each country, irrespective of industry, the necessary data must be created by summing the interactions within countries, across industries. When that is done, the ECIs for each country are determined by calculating for three-year, five-year, and seven-year periods what percentage the maximum number of interactions are of the total number of interactions in each country. Once again, however, the basic event underlying an ECI is interaction in a specific country in a specific three-digit industry.

An artificial example will make the point clear. Suppose that the maximum number of manufacturing subsidiaries established in Italy within any three-year period in each of three three-digit industries were as shown in Column 1 of the following table. Suppose further that the total number of subsidiaries formed in each of the three industries was as shown in Column 2.

SIC Code	(1) Maximum Interactions within Three Consecutive Years	(2) Total Interactions 1948–1967
201	4	8
281	6	9
291	3	4
Total	13	21

These figures would give Italy a three-year ECI of 13/21 or .618. In reality, of course, ECIs are based on interactions that take place within many more industries than the number in this illustration. But what is important to note is that the ECIs by country are not based upon firms that have set up subsidiaries in, say, SIC 201 interacting with firms that have set up subsidiaries in SIC 281 or 291; that is, apples are not mixed with oranges, one industry is not mixed with another. Rather, the interactions that matter are those that took place in each three-digit industry.

The ECIs for 21 of the 23 countries in the sample are presented in Appendix B. In the case of the two remaining countries, Luxembourg and Norway, there were too few inter-actions to permit computation of their ECIs.

Intercorrelation among ECIs by country.—In a number of tests reported in this chapter, only the average ECI by country was used. Since it was highly positively correlated with the other ECIs by country, there was little to be gained by work-ing with all the ECIs.

Intercorrelation among the ECIs by country gave the results shown in Table 8-1.

TABLE 8-1

Pearson Coefficients of Intercorrelation of ECIs by Country
(N = 21)

	3-year ECI	5-year ECI	7-year ECI	Average ECI
3-year ECI	+1.00	+ .69	+ .79	+ .89
5-year ECI		+1.00	+ .78	+ .92
7-year ECI			+1.00	+ .94
Average ECI				+1.00

NOTE: All coefficients are statistically significant at the .001 level.

Relationship between ECIs and number of subsidiaries by country.—Before getting into the heart of this chapter, i.e., the influence of market size, growth, and stability on interdepend-ent firm behavior, it is necessary to put to rest the possibility that the ECIs by country simply measure the number of sub-sidiaries established within each country. At first glance sev-eral of the findings about to be examined raise this possibility. Consider, for instance, these two findings: (1) the ECIs by country are positively related to various economic aggregates and to a measure of market attractiveness, and (2) U.S. firms have set up more manufacturing subsidiaries in large foreign markets than in small ones. Is it not fair then to ask whether the ECIs by country measure only the total inflow of manufacturing subsidiaries? The answer, which is no, is supported by the evidence below.

Simple correlation of the ECIs by country with the number of manufacturing subsidiaries that were established in each country during various time periods gave the results shown in Table 8-2.[7]

TABLE 8-2

Pearson Coefficients of Correlation of ECIs by Country with Number of Subsidiaries Formed by Country
(N = 19)

ECIs	Pre-1946	Number of Subsidiaries Formed 1946–1967	1958–1967	Pre-1968
3-year	−.14 (.282)	−.13 (.293)	−.02 (.461)	−.14 (.278)
5-year	−.32 (.090)	−.33 (.084)	−.25 (.154)	−.34 (.079)
7-year	−.15 (.274)	−.09 (.350)	.00 (.499)	−.12 (.314)
Average	−.24 (.166)	−.22 (.184)	−.12 (.319)	−.23 (.168)

Notice the level of statistical significance of many of these coefficients. One only can conclude that there is either no relationship between the ECIs and the number of subsidiaries formed by country or a weak negative relationship. The explanation for the negative relationship is that the greater the number of subsidiaries established in a country, the higher the denominator in the equation for computing the ECIs. Yet, this higher number of subsidiaries in no way would affect the numerator in the equation unless interaction took place. Putting it another way, if there is an increase in the number of subsidiaries formed in a country, this does not mean that interaction automatically will become more intense in that country. It follows that the possibility of the systematic bias, i.e., more subsidiaries equals higher ECIs, can be rejected.

---

[7] The number of subsidiary formations was taken from Vaupel and Curhan, *The Making of International Enterprise*. Although the ECIs by country were computed for 21 countries, this test, as well as several that follow, was based upon 19 countries only because the data had to be adapted to that presented in Vaupel and Curhan.

III. Correlation Results

Correlation of ECIs by country with economic aggregates.—
The effects of market size and market growth on entry concentration were analyzed by correlating the average ECI by country with the following economic aggregates: (1) total gross domestic product as of 1958 and as of 1963, (2) absolute increment in gross domestic product in the years 1958–1963 and 1958–1966, (3) gross domestic product per capita as of 1958 and as of 1963, (4) growth rate (1950–1960) in total gross domestic product, and (5) growth rate (1950–1960) in gross domestic product per capita.

Collectively these aggregates embodied data for almost all the twenty years covered by the study. It was assumed therefore that any relationships that would result from using these aggregates would not be significantly different from those that might be found by using these same aggregates measured at other points in time.

Because the correlation results would be obscured if the data included countries that had high per capita income but small total market size, the correlations were rerun, first excluding and then including Denmark and New Zealand, the two countries in the sample that were the most notable examples of this kind of imbalance between per capita income and total market size. The results are given in Table 8-3.

Since there was no *a priori* reason to expect that the average ECI by country would vary with changes over the whole range of values of the economic aggregates (indeed, it was more sensible to expect that the ECI might be insensitive to extreme values), these correlations were rerun again, this time employing the Spearman ranking technique, and the results are shown in Table 8-4.

Notice that in both sets of correlation results the presence or absence of data for Denmark and New Zealand affected the results in the way that one might expect.

Notice also that with or without data for these two countries

TABLE 8-3

Pearson Coefficients of Correlation of Average ECI by Country with Aggregate Measures of Market Size and Market Growth*

	Including Denmark and New Zealand (N = 21)	Excluding Denmark and New Zealand (N = 19)
Total GDP (1958)	+.04 (.439)	+.24 (.163)
Total GDP (1963)	+.09 (.342)	+.31 (.096)
Absolute Growth in Total GDP:		
(1958–1963)	+.20 (.196)	+.42 (.035)
(1958–1966)	+.20 (.187)	+.44 (.029)
GDP per Capita (1958)	+.36 (.056)	+.21 (.195)
GDP per Capita (1963)	+.45 (.022)	+.30 (.105)
Growth Rate in GDP (1950–1960)	−.10 (.355)	+.08 (.367)
Growth Rate in GDP per Capita (1950–1960)	+.24 (.148)	+.46 (.023)

* Data were adapted from United Nations, *Statistical Yearbook, 1968.* Gross Domestic Product was measured at factor cost.

TABLE 8-4

Spearman Coefficients of Correlation of Average ECI by Country with Aggregate Measure of Market Size and Market Growth

	Including Denmark and New Zealand (N = 21)	Excluding Denmark and New Zealand (N = 19)
Total GDP (1958)	−.06 (.391)	+.21 (.198)
Total GDP (1963)	+.01 (.496)	+.24 (.159)
Absolute Growth in Total GDP:		
(1958–1963)	+.15 (.252)	+.35 (.072)
(1958–1966)	+.15 (.258)	+.41 (.042)
GDP per Capita (1958)	+.33 (.070)	+.21 (.198)
GDP per Capita (1963)	+.44 (.023)	+.34 (.077)
Growth Rate in GDP (1950–1960)	−.11 (.312)	+.06 (.400)
Growth Rate in GDP per Capita (1950–1960)	+.23 (.154)	+.44 (.030)

the correlation results show that entry concentration is more related to absolute changes in GDP and to changes in GDP per capita than to static measures of these aggregates. Total GDP by country, while its coefficients are generally positive, is a particularly poor indicator of entry concentration by country.

All in all, the evidence substantially supports the market-size and market-growth arguments set out in the preceding pages. Large market size alone is not sufficient to spark flurries of defensive investments. For U.S. oligopolists contemplating foreign direct investment, relatively stagnant markets, even large ones, seem to raise the specter of infighting over market shares. In such situations, firms follow one another abroad with prudence. Many of those supplying the slow growing markets through exports may simply be content to rely on this less risky way of keeping their foot in the foreign market.

Large prospective uncovered demand, or at least high prospective growth, needs to be on the horizon to induce U.S. investors to jump on the bandwagon. Anticipating growth, U.S. firms will apparently accept the risks and uncertainties inherent in committing assets overseas for the purpose of offsetting the moves of rivals. Without growth, the game may not be worth the candle.

IV. Regression Results

Regression of ECIs by country on country variables.—Another step in determining the effects of market characteristics (including stability) on entry concentration was to regress the average ECIs by country on nine variables. Either the findings so far or the arguments presented in Section I of this chapter suggested that these nine might be associated with variation in the ECIs by country and might serve as independent variables in the regression analysis. The variables that were employed in one or more regressions were:

X_1 Total gross domestic product by country. Either total GDP for 1958 or for 1963 was used in the various regressions.

X_2 Gross domestic product per capita by country. Again, either 1958 or 1963 values were used.

X_3 Growth rate (1950–1960) in total GDP by country.

X_4 Growth rate (1950–1963) in GDP per capita by country.

X_5 The number of parent companies that first established a manufacturing subsidiary in a country before 1946, expressed as a percentage of the total number of parent companies that ever established a manufacturing subsidiary in the country. (In Chapter 4 this variable was used as one measure of oligopoly stability.)

X_6 Sherbini's economic-demographic index.

X_7 Sherbini's stability-cohesion index.

X_8 Average taxable foreign income per return by country for those U.S. corporations that reported income earned from foreign operations during the period July 1961–June 1962.[8]

X_9 Absolute increase in gross domestic product. Either increments for the years 1958–1963 or 1958–1966 were used in the regressions.

The average ECIs for 21 countries and for 19 countries (Denmark and New Zealand excluded) were regressed on various combinations of these variables.

Two of the variables listed above, Sherbini's indexes, need to be explained in some detail since they have not previously appeared in this study.

---

[8] These data, which can be viewed as the average profits of all manufacturing subsidiaries by country, were adjusted by subtracting from this average the average income for all manufacturing subsidiaries in SICs 29, 33, and 37. The highly integrated nature of the petroleum industry and of the basic metals industry meant that measures of profitability based only on the manufacturing segments of these industries significantly misrepresented profitability by country in these industries. The income earned by several overseas automobile manufacturing operations was so large relative to earnings by all other manufacturing operations that it badly distorted the average level of profitability of U.S. operations in certain countries.

This variable was shown subsequently to have no explanatory power. The data for this variable were developed from Internal Revenue Service, *Statistics of Income, 1962: Foreign Income and Taxes Reported on Corporation Income Tax Returns.*

Sherbini's indexes: two measures of "Investment Climate."—
In making their foreign investment decisions U.S. managements, quite naturally, have been sensitive to the characteristics of demand in foreign markets. The evidence in Section III
of this chapter bears this out. It is possible, however, that managements were even more sensitive to broad, general impres-
sions of market attractiveness than they were to estimates of
demand growth. In particular, they may have been lured by
markets that seemed to offer a high degree of overall socio-political stability. The reasons for this have already been spelled
out. Sherbini has devised indexes which measure two different
dimensions of what can best be called investment climate and
which can be used to test the stability proposition.[9]

Sherbini has calculated an economic-demographic index for
all leading countries. It is based on the following 21 indicators:

Development and Industrialization
   1. Per capita Gross National Product, U.S. dollars.
   2. Per capita commercial energy consumption (megawatt-
      hours).
Marketing Orientation
   1. Commercial sector as a percentage of the labor force.
Communications
   1. Per capita newsprint consumption (kilogrammes).
   2. Newspaper circulation per 1,000 population.
   3. Radio receivers per 1,000 population.
   4. Telephones per 1,000 population.
Transportation
   1. Motor vehicle density: vehicles per 100 kilometers of
      roads.
   2. Road density: kilometers per 100,000 population.
   3. Railway density: kilometers per person to population dis-
      tance.

---

[9] A. A. Sherbini, "Part Two: Classifying and Comparing Countries," in Bertil Lian-
der (ed.), *Comparative Analysis for International Marketing* (Boston: Allyn and Bacon, Inc.,
1967).

    4. Intensity of railway use: million freight ton-kilometers per railway kilometer.

Organization of Population

    1. Percentage of active population in agricultural occupations.

    2. Percentage of population in cities of 20,000 and more (urbanization).

    3. Population in largest city as a percentage of population in largest four cities (primacy).

Education

    1. Percentage of adults literate.

    2. Percentage of population aged 5–14 enrolled in primary level of education.

    3. Percentage of population aged 15–19 enrolled in secondary level of education.

    4. Enrollment in higher education per 100,000 population.

Health

    1. Inhabitants per hospital.

    2. Inhabitants per physician.

    3. Crude death rate.

Sherbini ranked countries on the basis of their total score for these 21 indicators, the data for which covered the years falling in the middle of the time period covered by this study, i.e., the late 1950s and early 1960s. His classification of markets should therefore approximate the ranking of foreign markets that managements might or could have made during this time period.

For our purposes, it is not necessary to go into how Sherbini manipulated the data to create his index—the reader who wishes details is referred to the original text—but to note that his index is a broader measure of the general economic development and sophistication of markets than are the economic aggregates used earlier in this chapter.

Sherbini's stability-cohesion index was designed to measure the internal stability and cohesion of a market and was based upon three indicators:

1. Deaths from domestic group violence (1950–1962) per 100,000 population.
2. Cultural homogeneity or fragmentation: an assessment of the extent to which each nation was racially, religiously, and linguistically homogeneous or heterogeneous.
3. The duration of national identity: a measure of the number of years each country had been sovereign.

As "catch-all" indexes, these two of Sherbini's are subject to many qualifications and limitations. Nonetheless, when managements were faced with making decisions about overseas investments or about countering the overseas investments of rivals, they quite likely organized their assessments of the many complexities and risks involved into rather crude ranking systems akin to the two Sherbini indexes.

Regression results.—Multiple regression of the average ECIs for the 21 countries on the nine independent variables produced an R^2 of .60; regression of the average ECIs for the 19 countries on the same variables produced an R^2 of .67. Although both regression equations were significant at the .01 level, few of the regression coefficients approached levels of acceptable statistical significance. This was to be expected, however, owing to multicollinearity among a number of the variables.

Stepwise regressions were therefore run; and whether data for Denmark and New Zealand were included or not, the Sherbini stability-cohesion index routinely entered the equations on the first step, and the variable representing oligopoly stability (X_5) routinely entered the equations on the second step. In subsequent steps the economic aggregates showed limited explanatory power. The variable measuring the average earnings of subsidiaries in each country also proved to be of little value. In no equation did the coefficient for this variable approach acceptable statistical significance; moreover, it usually took the negative sign, a result that was contrary to expec-

TABLE 8-5

Regression Equations for Average ECI by Country

Dependent Variable	Intercept	Independent Variables	R^2	F Ratio
ECI (21 countries)	.564	$+ .01361X_7$ (.00665) $- .00336X_5$ (.00147) $+ .00004X_2$ (1963) (.00003)	.49	5.34
ECI (19 countries)	.590	$+ .01199X_7$ (.00439) $- .00391X_5$ (.00121) $+ .00115X_1$ (1958) (.00085)	.59	7.24

NOTE: Both equations were significant at the .01 level. Figures in parentheses below the coefficients are the standard errors of the coefficients. All additional coefficients were not significantly different from zero at the .05 level.

tations. The results of the stepwise regressions are given in Table 8-5.

The addition of a third variable in these equations (per capita GDP in the first equation and total GDP in the second) increased the R^2 by .04 and .05 respectively; that is, they added little to the explanation of variation among the ECIs by country once the Sherbini stability-cohesion index and the variable representing oligopoly stability had been taken into account.

When Sherbini's stability-cohesion index was not included as an independent variable, the quality of the regression results deteriorated. For example, when the average ECIs for 21 countries were regressed on all the independent variables, excluding Sherbini's indexes, the first independent variable to enter the equation was GDP per capita for 1963, and the R^2 for the equation was .20. With Sherbini's indexes included as independent variables, the first to enter the equation was his stability-cohesion index, and the R^2 for the equation was .32.

The results were comparable when the average ECIs for only 19 countries were regressed on formulations that excluded and included Sherbini's indexes.

The stability-cohesion index and the economic aggregates.— One explanation for the importance of the Sherbini stability-cohesion index is that it served as a proxy for the economic aggregates. Correlation of the economic aggregates with Sherbini's stability-cohesion index and with his economic-demographic index resulted in fairly strong positive relationships.

TABLE 8-6

Pearson Coefficients of Correlation of Sherbini's Indexes with Economic Aggregates

	21 Countries			19 Countries		
	Total GDP (1958)	GDP/Capita (1958)	Δ GDP (1958–1963)	Total GDP (1958)	GDP/Capita (1958)	Δ GDP (1958–1963)
Stability-Cohesion Index	+.44(.024)	+.58(.003)	+.44(.023)	+.52(.012)	+.56(.007)	+.51(.013)
Economic-Demographic Index	+.43(.027)	+.88(.001)	+.33(.074)	+.51(.012)	+.88(.001)	+.40(.046)

Both indexes related equally with total GDP and roughly equally with the absolute gain in total GDP. But of the two the economic-demographic index showed the stronger positive association with GDP per capita. Now, if Sherbini's two indexes had functioned merely as surrogates for the economic aggregates in the regressions, his economic-demographic index would have been as good or better in explanatory power than his stability-cohesion index. Instead, in the regression equations, the coefficient for the economic-demographic index was signed negatively and was not statistically significant, and the coefficient associated with the stability-cohesion index had the most explanatory power of any of the coefficients associated with the independent variables. From this we can draw the conclusion that the stability-cohesion index is a measure of influences that lie outside the usual economic parameters, and that these influences have led to variation among the ECIs.

What the regression results point out is precisely what was argued in Section I of this chapter. By showing a positive relationship between the intensity of oligopolistic reaction and country stability, they indicate that oligopolists were not inclined to make defensive investments in unstable markets.

ECIs by country and oligopoly stability.—The only other independent variable that exhibited significant explanatory power in the regression equations was the number of U.S. parent companies that first established a manufacturing subsidiary in a country before 1946, expressed as a percentage of the total number of parent companies that ever established manufacturing subsidiaries in the country. This variable was negatively related to the ECIs by country in the same way that it was negatively related to the ECIs by industry and for the same reasons. (See Chapter 4.)

V. Market Size and Entry Concentration by Industry

Were the ECIs by industry subject to market-size bias?—The effect of market size on entry concentration by industry needs to be considered, for if it could be shown that the ECIs by industry were subject to significant market-size bias, then the variation found among the ECIs by industry would disappear if market size were held constant. Since to a limited extent large markets are associated with high ECIs by country (see Tables 8-3 and 8-4), the critical question is whether the data show that in general the ECIs by industry are systematically biased by a propensity of firms in some industries to expand into comparatively large markets only.

The issue raised here would have been resolved quite easily had it been possible to construct ECIs by industry, by country. But it was not possible (see Chapter 2), and hence it was necessary to rely on rather crude measures of the effects of market size on ECIs by industry.

Testing for market-size bias.—The measures for the effects of market size on the ECIs by industry and the test for bias were developed in the following manner.

1. A count by two-digit industry for the 12 international industries was made of the number of manufacturing subsidiaries that were established in 15 countries—a cross-section of the 23 countries in the sample.
2. The 15 countries were ranked on the basis of three measures of market size or market growth: (1) 1958 gross domestic product, (2) 1958 gross domestic product per capita, and (3) growth rate (1950–1960) in gross domestic product.[10]
3. On the basis of the above measures, the 15 countries were grouped for rank order 1–5, 6–10, and 11–15. The three groups were:

	Ranked by 1958 GDP	*Ranked by 1958 GDP per capita*	*Ranked by Growth Rate (1950–1960) in GDP*
The Five Highest Ranking Countries (not ranked within groups)	U.K.	U.K.	Mexico
	France	Switzerland	Venezuela
	Germany	France	Germany
	Italy	Germany	Japan
	Japan	Venezuela	Philippines
The Five Second Ranking Countries	Mexico	Argentina	Brazil
	Argentina	Italy	Peru
	Brazil	Netherlands	Colombia
	Netherlands	Spain	Italy
	Spain	Japan	Netherlands
The Five Lowest Ranking Countries	Peru	Mexico	Argentina
	Colombia	Brazil	U.K.
	Venezuela	Peru	Switzerland
	Switzerland	Colombia	France
	Philippines	Philippines	Spain

---

[10] Taken from United Nations, *Statistical Yearbook*, 1968.

4. A total was determined for the number of manufacturing subsidiaries that were established by two-digit industry within each of the three groups of countries shown above, and these totals were expressed as a percentage of the total number of subsidiaries formed in all 15 countries.
5. These percentages of subsidiaries formed by industries in the three groups of countries were correlated with the ECIs for the 12 two-digit international industries.

As to correlation results, it was expected that if industries with high ECIs had a tendency to establish a disproportionately high percentage of their subsidiaries in large or rapidly growing markets, then there would be a positive correlation between the ECIs and the percentage of subsidiaries established in these markets and a negative correlation between the ECIs and the percentage of subsidiaries established in countries with small or low growth-rate markets.

For the 12 two-digit industries, correlation of their ECIs (three-year, five-year, and seven-year ECIs and average ECI) with the percentages of total subsidiaries formed by each of the industries in the nine groups of countries generated 36 correlation coefficients that exhibited no pattern whatever; they took positive or negative signs in a random manner; their values, regardless of sign, were generally quite low; and only two out of the 36 were statistically significant at the .05 level.

These results do not support the supposition that some industries made a high proportion of all their direct investments in large or rapidly growing markets, whereas others made a high proportion of all their direct investments in small or slowly growing markets. To the contrary, large markets apparently attracted direct investment and small markets apparently deterred direct investment to the same degree irrespective of industry. If, therefore, variation among the ECIs by industry does not reflect market-size bias, it seems safe to conclude that the variation reflects differences in industry structures and in industry characteristics. This conclusion is, of course, the gist of all the preceding chapters.

VI. Entry Concentration: Independent or Interdepend ent Behavior?

The evidence in this chapter that the ECIs are positively related to market growth opens the door on a final issue that calls for attention lest the door swing wide open. The problem is posed by a model of the foreign investment process that is at odds with the one underlying this study. The alternative model rejects the whole notion of oligopolistic reaction. Instead, it proposes something like the following. Suppose rival firms make decisions to invest abroad independent of one another and, by and large, strictly on the basis of perceived gains in foreign demand. Then if, for one reason or another, the ability of firms in one industry to move abroad differ from that of firms in another industry, there could be variation between the two in entry concentration. But the variation would have nothing to do with interdependent investment behavior.

Note that the independent behavior point of view rests upon the presumption of the existence of another fundamental factor, other than oligopolistic reaction, that varies from one industry to the next and that influences either the willingness or the ability of firms to engage in foreign direct investment. The factor must be an all-encompassing one, for if it is to take the place of oligopolistic reaction, it must explain all the findings already reviewed up to this point. The next several pages constitute a search for this "other factor."

Let us start with what could be called organizational efficiency. Suppose firms in tightly structured oligopolies were better managed, in some general sense, than those in less concentrated oligopolies. Suppose, in particular, that one consequence of this better management was rapid decision-making ability. Then, when new market opportunities were perceived, member firms in tight oligopolies could act promptly; a flurry of direct investments might follow. But in the less concentrated industries, where decision making was a slow and not altogether efficient process, responses would be scattered; little clustering of investments would take place. In terms of the measures used in this study, entry concentration would be positively associated with industry concentration, yet the causal link would not be oligopolistic reaction.

Though the idea of differences among industries in decision-making capabilities is a plausible one, it is hard to reconcile the implications of the notion for empirical findings with the actual findings of this study. For if it were more or less correct, then there ought to be a positive relationship between ECIs by industry and measures of market attractiveness. However, we have just seen in Section V of this chapter that the ECIs by industry are unrelated to market variables. Recall that all industries seem to move rapidly into growth markets and to move with some hesitation into nongrowth markets. There is no indication that some industries consistently seize new foreign market opportunities more vigorously than others. To be sure, the test in Section V used crude tools, but if something like organizational efficiency was a persistent and fundamental factor, there should have been some evidence of it at work. No such evidence appeared.

Suppose the issue turns not so much on organizational efficiency as on organizational experience. Certainly U.S. managements setting up their tenth manufacturing subsidiary overseas have an experience edge over those setting up their first or second subsidiary abroad. And some industries may be predominantly dominated by experienced firms, others by relatively novice firms. Though their decisions were independently arrived at, experienced firms might still invest abroad *en masse* at the first sign of a new foreign market opportunity. Not so for the novices.

Like the first argument, this second undoubtedly identifies an element that has had some part in molding the foreign investment behavior of U.S. industry. But, again, it is hard to make the argument jibe with the facts. If firms gain experience by setting up subsidiaries, and subsequently move abroad in lock-step with rivals simply because of the experience advantage, there ought to be a positive relationship between the number of subsidiaries established by industry and the ECIs by industry. Neither the evidence in Chapter 3 (which pertained to ECIs by industry) nor the evidence in Chapter 8 (which pertained to ECIs by country) demonstrated such a relationship. If anything, the ECIs are negatively related to the number of subsidiaries set up by industry in the pre- and in the post-World War II years. Though these findings do not dismiss the experience argument altogether, they clearly raise serious doubts about its validity.

Perhaps different investment patterns in high-risk and low-risk foreign countries have been the underlying operative factor. Consider the implications for the findings of the following assumed chain of events. Suppose that in the pre-World War II years the member firms in some industries made a number of investments in the commonly regarded stable countries, say in the U.K., in several members of the Commonwealth, and in one or two of the principal continental markets. Postwar, having little need to establish additional subsidiaries in these countries, the firms in these industries directed most of their investment efforts toward some of the less stable markets. Possibly, less-developed countries were their common investment targets. Now, because the risks and uncertainties associated with investing in this second tier of countries would be perceived as high, U.S. companies would move into these markets only with great circumspection. Investors would seldom flock in; concentrated entry would seldom occur.

But in other industries, newcomers to international expansion, postwar foreign investment may have been focused principally on the stable developed countries where risks and uncertainties were not so great. Firms could be somewhat less circumspect. At the first sign of market opportunities, U.S. investors would move with little hesitation. Concentrated entry patterns would result.

What is being postulated here is that variation among industries in entry concentration could be the result of the historical sequence in which industries moved into sets of markets with different risk and uncertainty characteristics. Had this study included in its sample base data from a substantial number of less-developed countries, it is certainly possible that this argument might have identified an important source of bias in the findings. But most of the countries included in the sample base were those that, by most standards, would be regarded as stable developed ones. Moreover, once again, the argument, does not fit the facts.

Of the sampled countries, the block of Latin American ones most closely falls into the high-risk and uncertainty category. If the foregoing argument was correct, then there should be evidence of a negative relationship between the ECIs by industry and the proportion of subsidiaries established postwar by industry in the Latin American countries. Tests demonstrate no such relationship. Apparently market stability affects oligopolistic behavior like market growth. All industries are more or less equally attracted to stable or growing markets. Without some initial evidence that variation among the ECIs by industry can be attributed to different patterns of investing in high-risk markets, there is no reason to expect that this factor would explain all the rest of the results in the study.

Scale could be a contender for the "other factor." After all, scale is positively associated with industry concentration. Interdependency aside, scale constraints—the balance needed between scale requirements and the size of demand in foreign markets—might account for variation by industry in the ECIs. But in Chapter 6 we saw that little could be explained about the ECIs, especially the three-year and five-year ECIs, by scale factors. In one industry after the next, the leading firms seem to ignore scale considerations in the quest to perpetuate equilibria.

At this point it is useful to raise the question whether any set of tests or observations can conclusively settle the matter of interdependency or independency. Probably not. But then the intent of the few preceding pages was not to "settle" with finality anything. Research does not progress when the investigator's point of view is to put issues to rest. Nor was the intent to dismiss, in checklist-like fashion, the general validity of all the foregoing arguments. Clearly all the factors discussed above have influenced in one way or another how U.S. investors have moved abroad. Nonetheless, they apparently fail to supplant oligopolistic reaction as the fundamental explanation for the specific evidence of this inquiry.

A concluding thought on this matter. Recall from Chapter 1 the following two points. U.S. businessmen say that they have made their foreign direct investment decisions with an eye on what their rivals were doing. Oligopoly theory's notion of interdependency leads us to expect that this would have been the case. The many empirical findings of this study consistently support the view that this has been so.

9
Conclusion

I. Recapitulation

As far as analysis goes, what can be said has been said. This final chapter will not probe further the chessboard world of oligopolists. Instead, its first aim is to provide the reader with a concise summary of the principal findings of this study. Then, its purpose is to examine briefly how the findings bear upon two other related issues:

1. We have seen that oligopolistic reaction influences how a good many U.S. enterprises invest abroad in advanced countries. What are the implications of oligopolistic reaction for investment in less-developed countries?

2. We have seen that many U.S. enterprises have evolved or are evolving into international oligopolists. How will they interact with large non-U.S. based firms on the same evolutionary path? Are long-lived multinational oligopolies, composed of firms of different nationalities, in the offing?

Regarding this second issue, prediction is not the object. Rather, the findings prompt a series of questions about the nature of interdependency among multinational firms confronting one another in multiple market places. The intent therefore is to use the findings to elaborate some of the topics that are likely to be the subject of future reasearch on the competitive environment of the multinational firm.

Drawing to a close.—Briefly put, what have we seen? Chapter 1 made the case for oligopolistic reaction by developing a risk-minimizing model of foreign investment behavior among product-pioneering firms. They contest one another in foreign markets, so the argument went, in order to protect the exploitability abroad of the special technological and organizational capabilities they previously acquired at home. Product-pioneering industries are oligopolies. As a general rule, therefore, the higher the seller concentration in each industry, the hotter the contest. And since the risks of not offsetting the foreign moves of near rivals can exceed the risks of making parallel moves, product pioneers hedge by turning to the strategy of checkmating foreign direct investment.

As all the subsequent chapters demonstrated, firms with few alternatives pursued this strategy vigorously. Those with a number of alternative ways to protect their interests abroad or to establish new stakes abroad pursued this strategy sporadically if at all.

These broad conclusions were reached by examining how the bunching of U.S. industry's foreign direct investments, measured by the entry concentration indexes (the ECIs), has been related to firm, industry, and country characteristics. What did that examination bring to light?

Summary of findings.—The findings of the analysis may be summarized as follows:

1. Entry concentration is not a matter of conjecture; it is a matter of fact. Data from a sample of 187 U.S. parent companies show that almost half of their foreign manufacturing subsidiaries established sometime during 1948–1967 in any given industry and country under study were established in three-year peak clusters; almost three-fourths were established in seven-year peak clusters.

There is some evidence, hardly conclusive to be sure, that neither random events nor the overall trend of U.S. investment abroad accounts for the bunching of foreign direct investments. That this matter cannot be resolved conclusively is the result of applying a rigorous test—using randomized ECIs weighted by the overall investment trend—that may have been biased by the very phenomenon being tested.

2. Generally speaking, entry concentration is positively related to industry concentration. ECIs at the three-digit and two-digit industry levels are positively correlated with four-firm and eight-firm concentration ratios. This is also true in the case of three-digit industries within two-digit industries. The positive correlation is, in all instances, strongest with the three-year ECIs. Thus, with an exception to be noted in a moment, firms pursue the strategy of defensive investment more actively in industries of high seller concentration than in industries of low seller concentration. Also, the countering of rivals' foreign direct investments seems to be most energetic in those industries in which marketing is the dominant corporate activity. Finally, the positive link between entry concentration and seller concentration is mainly determined by the behavior of the few leading firms in each industry.

3. Though the intensity of defensive investment is positively linked to the level of seller concentration in many industries, this is not the case in all industries. U.S. parent firms in industries with very high seller concentration (eight-firm concentration ratios above 70%) tend to interact less intensively than those in less concentrated industries because in the former ones high firm interdependency is coupled with high structural stability. Newcomer firms have rarely challenged the international expansion moves of the traditional rivals in these industries. But in industries that are not very highly concentrated or exceptionally stable, active rivalry among traditional members, stimulated by new entrants, leads to brisk defensive investment.

Tests employing weighted randomized ECIs conclusively demonstrate that the statistical findings underlying the foregoing conclusions cannot be explained by random events or by the overall trend in U.S. industry's investment overseas. Furthermore, the values of the ECIs are not biased by the absolute number of U.S. parent firms that have entered any industry abroad or by the number of overseas subsidiaries that have been established by industry.

4. By industry, entry concentration is negatively related to overseas product diversity. Thus the intensity of checkmating investment is in part determined by the breadth of a firm's product line. Narrow product-line firms, because they have few options, tend to respond in kind when a rival makes a foreign direct investment. Wide product-line firms, on the other hand, because they have the capacity to exploit foreign markets in a variety of ways, are not as inclined to oligopolistic reaction.

5. The few leaders of each industry, those that react swiftly to one another's moves, tend to ignore scale considerations when they invest abroad. Followers, on the other hand, are often dissuaded from swiftly countering the moves of rivals by such factors as the magnitude of the investment or the lack of accord between corporate capabilities and the risks and uncertainties involved in investing overseas. These conclusions flow from the finding that the five-year and seven-year ECIs, but not the three-year ECIs, are negatively correlated with measures of scale.

The ECIs are also negatively correlated with R&D expenditures as a percentage of sales and with advertising expenditures as a percentage of sales. Innovation and product differentiation, like diversification, seem to generate options that free firms from slavishly mimicking the moves of rivals.

6. The profitability of overseas manufacturing industries is positively related to entry concentration. This is particularly so in the case of the very prompt interaction. The direction of causality in this relationship is unclear. On the one hand, firms in generally profitable industries can best afford the resources required for prompt defensive investment. On the other hand, prompt defensive investment by sets of traditional rivals may have the effect of re-establishing abroad oligopolistic behavior patterns that proved profitable back home. Though the evidence on the matter is compatible with either point of view, the specific statistical findings cannot be com-

pletely and adequately explained unless the second cause is at least partially at work.

7. Entry concentration by industry is positively related to measures of market growth much more so than it is to measures of market size. Expectations about future demand apparently figure more heavily in foreign investment decisions than do perceptions of existing demand.

Regression results show that environmental stability is a particularly important determinant of variation among the ECIs. Near rivals counter one another's moves willingly under relatively stable circumstances; not so under unstable ones.

The ECIs are not affected by market-size bias. Nor are they affected by a number of other general factors, e.g., organizational experience, that might have explained the findings of this study instead of oligopolistic reaction.

All these findings were based upon data relating to, with only a few exceptions, advanced nations. Are there any messages here for the less-developed countries?

II. Implications for Less-Developed Countries

When less-developed countries (LDCs) turn to the West for help in developing their economies, but are reluctant to turn to private enterprise for assistance, the reason may be that they believe they lack the power to bargain with the industrial oligopolies of the West.

The LDC's position.—To the individual LDC the problem may look like this: A few large firms control the technology or bundle of skills the LDC needs. As a result of oligopolistic interdependence, these firms have reached a commonly held conclusion about the international value of their technology or skills; and until the products that have resulted from these technologies reach the later stages of their product life cycles, they are likely to have oligopolistically determined market prices. The oligopolists will regard the value of their technology as directly related to these prices.

Although in the eyes of the LDC the value that the oligopolists have placed on their technology, either in terms of selling it outright or in terms of making a direct investment in the LDC, may seem far too excessive, it undoubtedly realizes that if it shops around for "fire sales" of technology, it is unlikely to be successful. Should one oligopolist underprice the technology, it could anticipate retaliation from its rivals.

Out of the frying pan into the fire.—Another reason the LDC may hesitate to turn to oligopolists for technology is that it fears the possibility of export market foreclosure. While the LDC knows that some industries, those whose products have a high labor content, will transfer technology to it because they want to benefit from low costs of production and to use the LDC as an export base, the LDC also knows that other industries, though they may be willing to transfer technology, may decide not to use the LDC as an export base.

If, then, to sidestep this possibility, the LDC buys the technology outright, it is still faced with the possibility that the export markets for the products of this technology are so tightly controlled by the original owners of the technology that they are closed to the LDC.

Though the LDC may believe that regardless of the circumstances it will get the worst end of any bargain it makes with oligopolists, this need not be the case. Should it become sensitive to what motivates oligopolists, it would have the necessary power to deal with them effectively. The following suggestions are directed at LDCs, and although they are by no means new, their worth is given additional support by the findings of this study.[1]

Oligopolistic reaction: a trump card for the LDC.—As soon as the LDC allows one member of a foreign oligopoly to set up a

---

[1] The ideas for some of these suggestions were taken from a report prepared in 1970 by Professor Raymond Vernon for the government of Indonesia.

local manufacturing facility, it may expect that the other members will want "in" as well. Then the balance of bargaining power has shifted to the side of the LDC. Moreover, if it is dealing with a concentrated oligopoly, it will have more bargaining power still because of the tendency of firms in such industries to interact intensively. When one member of the club makes a move, the others pant to follow; and by realizing this, the LDC is in a position to demand a high entrance fee. What the LDC can do is attract one leader in each industry by means of fairly strong inducements and then plan on hard bargaining with any of the others that wish to follow.

Enticing the outsiders.—The preceding suggestion for the LDC needs to be qualified to this extent: It may not work if the LDC is negotiating with the member firms of a highly concentrated, stable oligopoly. As we have seen, the *modus vivendi* that firms reach under such conditions sharply diminishes oligopolistic reaction.

Yet the LDC need not be powerless in this situation, for the evidence (Chapter 4) suggests that there is nothing like a new rival to bring to life oligopolistic reaction. If the LDC can entice a firm that is not a member of an oligopoly to invest within its borders for the purpose of manufacturing the oligopoly's products, the LDC's bargaining position vis-à-vis the traditional oligopoly members is likely to improve. The established oligopolists may then be eager to bargain over terms of entry.

Some LDCs seem to have learned this lesson already. Indonesia is a case in point. Bent on developing a local copper industry, the Indonesian government first granted Freeport Sulphur, an industry outsider, investment rights with fairly liberal terms attached. Subsequently, the Indonesian government approved an investment proposal by Kennecott Copper, but the terms of this agreement were apparently less liberal than those negotiated with Freeport Sulphur. Clearly, Indonesia was playing the outsider against the insider.

Do more investors mean more competition?—In its desire to encourage competition among oligopolists, the LDC may regard it wise to attract direct investments by three or four firms in an oligopoly. But it is questionable whether such a policy will produce the desired results. As we have seen (Chapter 7), when the industry leaders in tight oligopolies rapidly counter one another's investments, they may emphasize the modes of competitive conduct that have proved profitable for them all; and these are not likely to include price competition.

If therefore the LDC hopes to narrow the gap between the private and social returns on the investments, it should keep in mind that an open door policy to investment by foreign oligopolists is not necessarily the road to this objective.

The road to inefficient production.—Another possible drawback to an open door policy is that it may encourage the formation of industries dominated by small-scale, inefficient plants. But the LDC need not learn this lesson firsthand. More advanced countries that have been the recipients of extensive foreign direct investment can serve as an example. As Donald Brash points out:

> . . . the combination of almost any actual or potential barrier to trade with the oligopolistic nature of most of the industries in which foreign investment is important tends to produce a great proliferation of small-scale foreign-owned units, without any real prospect of rationalization or consolidation. . . . If the units were domestically owned, one could expect market forces to bring about consolidation over a period; when they are owned by large internationally competing corporations, this is highly unlikely.[2]

The findings in Chapter 6 give additional support to Brash's argument. Recall that the early entrants into foreign countries

---

[2] Donald T. Brash, "Australia as a Host to the International Corporation," in Charles P. Kindleberger (ed.), *The International Corporation*, p. 317.

tend to overlook scale requirements; their first concern is to counter the moves of recognized rivals.

If, then, oligopolists that are quick to counter do ignore scale requirements, the LDC, should it follow an open door policy and not insist upon some minimum scale requirements, may well end up with some of its industries composed of inefficient small-scale foreign-owned plants.

Doubtless, policy planners in most LDCs already appreciate the points listed above. The findings in this study simply confirm that they are unlikely to formulate guidelines for attracting foreign investors, on terms favorable to investors and the hosts alike, unless they recognize the interfirm dependencies of the potential entrants.

III. Toward the Multinational Oligopoly in the Advanced Countries

From domestic to international oligopolies.—Roughly speaking, this analysis has examined the behavior of the U.S. product-pioneering industries while they were changing from domestic to international oligopolies in the advanced countries of the West. Although the findings that have been presented consistently support the notion that U.S. firms have made a substantial number of foreign direct investments with the aim of preventing industry rivals from gaining an upper hand, it is not an easy matter to predict from this what will happen in the future. Some prognosticators regard the trend toward multicountry oligopolies in the West as almost inevitable. On the basis of this study, however, it would seem that the issue is resistant to conclusive proof. Consider why.

From international to multinational oligopolies.—Hymer and Rowthorn, who have applied oligopoly concepts to an analysis of competition between leading U.S. and western European firms, see the future like this: Firms will take part in a process of cross-investment in the important national and international markets of each other, and this will lead to multinational market structures, each of which will be dominated by a few multinational firms and characterized by stable oligopolistic equilibrium.[3]

It may be presumptuous of this writer to do battle with Hymer and Rowthorn, but it needs pointing out that their estimate of the future seems to overlook the fact that some firms, in some industries, attach a good deal of importance to maintaining open a number of strategic options. The evidence presented in Chapter 5, which deals with the diversified firm, and the evidence presented in Chapter 6, which is concerned with the R&D-oriented firm, suggest that such enterprises may be unwilling to become full-fledged members of world-wide oligopolies because they put a high premium on deciding when and where they will use their resources. It is doubtful therefore whether market stability will ever be the overriding goal of such firms.

Moreover, the notion that an industry will reach world-wide market stability hinges upon the assumption that whatever the competitive capabilities of one firm, these can be balanced by the competitive capabilities of the others. But what is the effect when whatever accounts for competitive strengths changes? Obviously the balance is disrupted. And in today's world there seem to be more factors on the side of change than on the side of stability.

Furthermore, a forecast of a world in which industries are composed of a few giant firms all living in a state of restrained and profitable rivalry calls for some sweeping assumptions about the organizational behavior of the multinational firm. In particular it calls for the assumption that the multinational firm is a monolithic decision maker; yet the more one relaxes this assumption, the more difficult it becomes to predict multinational firm conduct.

---

[3] Stephen Hymer and Robert Rowthorn, "Multinational Corporations and International Oligopoly: The Non-American Challenge," in Kindleberger (ed.), pp. 81–82.

The preceding few paragraphs simply pose obstacles to forecasting the future for the multinational firm facing multinational rivals. The succeeding final section suggests some tentative ways to clarify that future.

IV. Unanswered Questions

Expanding the oligopoly model.—For the most part, oligopoly theory has been concerned with a one-product, one-country model, but if researchers are to get at the heart of the matter of the behavior of the multinational enterprise, they should be prepared to develop a multiproduct, multicountry model. Though this research is a step in that direction, it need hardly be said that it is a small step and a great many unsolved problems lie ahead. In particular, three topics suggest themselves for further investigation:

1. On what factor or resource or advantage have oligopolistic equilibria depended in the past and on what will they depend in the future?

2. What has been and what will be the nature of oligopolistic discipline across countries?

3. In what ways do the internal organization and managerial processes in the multinational firm affect the oligopolistic behavior of the firm?

Equilibrium of what?—One of the fundamental assumptions of this study is that the underlying motive for much of oligopolistic reaction among firms in product-pioneering industries is the protection of access to foreign markets and of share of business within the markets. The evidence we looked at in Chapter 3 appears to bear this out. Recall that member firms in marketing-oriented industries were far and away the most active defensive investors.

But if the study had been directed at another group of industries, say extractive industries, or if it had covered a different time period, say the foreseeable future, quite a different picture would have emerged. For firms in extractive industries, for instance, the battle is less likely to be over market access or share and more likely to be over access to raw materials.

And just as what constitutes competitive strength—i.e., the acquired technological and organizational capabilities referred to in Chapter 1—is not the same from one industry to another, neither is it likely to be the same from one time period to another. All matter and things are subject to time and change, and this includes what firms regard as the essential nature of their competitive strength.

Coming to the point, there are a number of reasons for believing that with regard to firms in some industries, the contest among member firms for market access and share may have become a secondary matter, at least as far as the economically developed countries are concerned.

Take the electronics industry, for example. In the last decade firms in the industry have moved to offshore production. And though they may still do battle with one another over market franchises in the United States and other economically developed countries, their ability to compete now appears to depend on how successful they are in developing cheap offshore production. Thus one may argue that in the future stability of equilibrium in this industry will hinge upon two conditions: that the firms in the industry can avoid mutually destructive rivalry in the market place and that they all can achieve a similar assortment of production facilities at home and abroad, so that all firms in the industry have the same range of production costs.

The intended implication here is that whereas in the past the big contest among firms focused on market access —where and when to set up subsidiaries—to preserve industry structure, in the future the contest may well be directed at matching one another's production cost curves on a worldwide basis. Further research will tell.

Maintaining an ordered market in multinational oligopoly.—
While it is undoubtedly true that to establish world-wide market order, firms in major or powerful oligopolies must undertake direct investments in each other's home markets and all other principal foreign markets, it is not necessarily true that such cross-investment will, in and of itself, lead to stability. Market order, when it arises, stems out of a process of trial and error among rivals in an industry. There are periods of stability and there are periods of aggressive rivalry, including sometimes active price competition. But even when stability is the existing state of affairs, it is anything but permanent. Hence, for oligopolistically structured industries, stable conditions in international markets will require an on-going process of member firms' disciplining one another.

The preceding statement raises an important question. How have multinational firms disciplined one another in the past and how may they discipline one another in the future? Let us consider the matter from the standpoint of an imaginary example. Suppose, for instance, that firm A, a U.S.-controlled multinational firm, and firm B, a German-controlled multinational firm, have large subsidiaries in each other's home country and in a number of other countries. Now suppose that A breaks the price in Germany on one of B's principal products. What should B do? Cut the price of this product in Germany; cut the price in some other important market, but not in the United States; cut the price in the United States; cut the price on another important product of A; or retaliate by some means other than price competition? The alternatives before B are, at the theoretical level, almost inexhaustible. In the real world, however, this is seldom the case.

So what are the facts of the matter? Has this kind of discipline across countries and across products actually taken place, or is it simply an issue of conjecture? The question needs answering.

*The effects of organization on oligopolistic behavior.—*There are two features of the multinational firm that raise questions about its ability to control the process that is necessary for it to reach tacit understanding with rivals in the industry. First, in any institution as widespread, many-layered, and multifaceted as the multinational enterprise, it is to be expected that communication of purpose and policy between corporate head-quarters and operating subunits will be far from exact. And second, if subunits, in particular foreign subsidiaries, are to succeed at their job, they require a high degree of autonomy. Management in the home office is scarcely in a position to know what is immediately demanded in order to deal effectively with exigencies that arise in its foreign markets from one day to the next.

The questions therefore are: (a) to what extent do subunits shape the conduct of the multinational firm and (b) how does the organizational structure or managerial practices of the multinational firm determine how subunits will deal with rivals? The two questions point to the competitive strategy dilemma that faces top management of the multinational firm.

On the one hand, top management no doubt wants to insure that its subunits will not engage in market practices that are in any way illegal either in terms of U.S. law or in terms of foreign law. But on the other hand, management may use its subsidiaries, as if they were pawns, when its purpose is to establish world-wide market order for its products.

All this implies that if management of a multinational firm has used subsidiaries as competitive weapons, it has had to deal with a number of organizational issues. Stated in the form of questions, these issues are:

1. How does management develop world-wide competitive strategies if, for example, pricing decisions are widely decentralized?

2. How does management reconcile measuring a subsidiary's performance against profit goals with the use of that subsidiary in the firm's implementation of world-wide competitive strategies?

3. If a firm is organized around world-wide product groups,

how does management induce one product group to take actions in a number of markets for the benefit of another product group?

4. How can a subsidiary be used to fight a local competitive battle if it is part of an integrated and rationalized world-wide production system?

All this is for the purpose of suggesting that effective multinational competitive strategies depend upon the ability of the firm to manipulate its competitive instruments, and how it should do this is a wide-open field for inquiry.

APPENDIXES

APPENDIX A

Entry Concentration Indexes by Industry

TABLE A-1

ECIs for Three-Digit Industries

SIC Code	Industry Title	Entry Concentration Indexes 3-year	5-year	7-year	average
201	Meat Products	.363	.545	.636	.515
202	Dairy Products	.552	.690	.793	.678
203	Canned, Cured, and Frozen Foods	.559	.765	.912	.745
204	Grain Mill Products	.477	.631	.738	.615
205	Bakery Products	.625	.667	.792	.695
206	Sugar	.667	.667	.667	.667
207	Confectionery and Related Products	.512	.683	.805	.667
208	Beverages	.400	.667	.733	.600
209	Misc. Foods and Kindred Products	.477	.705	.795	.659
264	Misc. Converted Paper Products	.483	.621	.793	.632
265	Paperboard Containers and Boxes	.400	.600	.771	.590
281	Industrial Chemicals	.456	.591	.694	.580
282	Plastics Materials and Synthetics	.477	.614	.745	.612
283	Drugs	.404	.551	.685	.547
284	Soap, Cleaners, and Toilet Goods	.486	.633	.697	.605
285	Paints and Allied Products	.480	.560	.760	.600
287	Agricultural Chemicals	.455	.606	.818	.626
289	Misc. Chemicals	.467	.633	.717	.606
291	Petroleum Refining	.523	.591	.659	.591
299	Misc. Petroleum and Coal Products	.500	.607	.857	.655
301	Tires and Inner Tubes	.286	.619	.619	.508
321	Flat Glass	.571	.571	.571	.571
329	Misc. Nonmetallic Mineral Products	.467	.622	.711	.600
333	Primary Nonferrous Metals	.556	.556	.667	.593
335	Nonferrous Rolling and Drawing	.667	1.000	1.000	.889
336	Nonferrous Foundries	.556	.556	.667	.593
341	Metal Cans	.444	.889	.889	.741
342	Cutlery, Hand Tools, and Hardware	.333	.733	.867	.644
343	Plumbing and Heating, Except Electrical	.250	.750	.875	.625

TABLE A-1—*Continued*

ECIs for Three-Digit Industries

SIC Code	Industry Title	3-year	5-year	7-year	average
344	Fabricated Structural Metal Products	.000	.333	.500	.278
348	Misc. Fabricated Wire Products	.833	1.000	1.000	.944
349	Misc. Fabricated Metal Products	.537	.667	.796	.667
351	Engines and Turbines	.500	.583	.917	.667
352	Farm Machinery	.500	.600	.700	.600
353	Construction and Related Machinery	.413	.540	.698	.550
355	Special Industry Machinery	.382	.529	.676	.529
356	General Industrial Machinery	.472	.583	.750	.602
357	Office and Computing Machines	.263	.684	.789	.579
358	Service Industry Machines	.600	.667	.867	.711
361	Electric Test and Distributing Equipment	.500	.750	.750	.667
362	Electrical Industrial Apparatus	.294	.412	.824	.510
363	Household Appliances	.500	.639	.750	.630
364	Electric Lighting and Wiring Equipment	.750	.917	1.000	.889
365	Radio and TV Receiving Equipment	.250	.250	.500	.333
366	Communication Equipment	.182	.455	.636	.424
367	Electronic Components and Accessories	.423	.808	.885	.705
369	Misc. Electrical Equipment and Supplies	.313	.625	.688	.542
371	Motor Vehicles and Equipment	.500	.640	.779	.640
372	Aircraft and Parts	.400	1.000	1.000	.800
381	Engineering and Scientific Instruments	.800	1.000	1.000	.933
382	Mechanical Measuring and Control Devices	.500	.500	.500	.500
384	Medical Instruments and Supplies	.438	.563	.813	.605
386	Photographic Equipment and Supplies	.500	.500	1.000	.667
399	Misc. Manufactures	.333	.611	.722	.555

TABLE A-2

Summary Statistics of ECIs for Three-Digit Industries
(N = 54)

	Mean	Range	Standard Deviation	Standard Error of the Mean
3-year ECI	.464	.833	.145	.020
5-year ECI	.644	.750	.151	.021
7-year ECI	.768	.500	.127	.017
Average ECI	.625	.666	.121	.016

TABLE A-3

Pearson Coefficients of Intercorrelation of ECIs for Three-Digit Industries
(N = 54)

	3-year ECI	5-year ECI	7-year ECI	Average ECI
3-year ECI	1.00	.59	.48	.81
5-year ECI		1.00	.75	.91
7-year ECI			1.00	.86
Average ECI				1.00

NOTE: All coefficients are statistically significant at the .001 level.

TABLE A-4

ECIs for Two-Digit Industries

SIC Code	Industry Title	Entry Concentration Indexes 3-year	5-year	7-year	average
20	Food and Kindred Products	.507	.678	.786	.656
26	Paper and Allied Products	.437	.609	.781	.609
28	Chemicals and Allied Products	.454	.595	.712	.587
29	Petroleum and Coal Products	.514	.598	.736	.616
30	Rubber and Plastics Products	.438	.563	.688	.563
32	Stone, Clay, and Glass Products	.632	.737	.789	.719
33	Primary Metal Industries	.600	.690	.800	.697
34	Fabricated Metal Products	.432	.710	.798	.647
35	Machinery, Except Electrical	.431	.579	.740	.584
36	Electrical Equipment and Supplies	.424	.642	.775	.615
37	Transportation Equipment	.500	.640	.779	.640
38	Instruments and Related Products	.516	.614	.806	.645

APPENDIX B

Entry Concentration Indexes by Country

TABLE B-1

ECIs by Country

Country	3-year	Entry Concentration Indexes 5-year	7-year	average
Argentina	.451	.597	.739	.596
Brazil	.418	.590	.707	.573
Colombia	.452	.606	.705	.589
Mexico	.382	.550	.690	.541
Peru	.480	.640	.760	.628
Venezuela	.418	.588	.736	.581
Belgium	.500	.598	.804	.635
Denmark	.667	.778	1.000	.817
France	.555	.715	.841	.703
Germany	.460	.603	.854	.640
Italy	.476	.656	.786	.641
Netherlands	.513	.713	.839	.690
Spain	.551	.678	.796	.676
Sweden	.500	.649	.678	.609
Switzerland	.421	.790	.790	.669
United Kingdom	.412	.552	.685	.550
South Africa	.314	.463	.569	.450
Australia	.453	.543	.701	.565
New Zealand	.688	.688	.812	.731
Japan	.533	.750	.831	.705
Philippines	.424	.558	.692	.559

APPENDIX C

Aggregation of ECIs and Industry Concentration Ratios

Creating ECIs at the two-digit industry level.–Initially, ECIs were calculated for industries at the SIC three-digit level. Because, however, data collected by the U.S. Government on the international operations of U.S. industry are often reported at the two-digit industry level only, in a number of statistical tests it was necessary to use data, and these included the ECIs, at this gross level of aggregation.

ECIs at the two-digit level were calculated for the 12 international industries[1] in one of two ways. In some instances they were based upon the sum of all interactions for all three-digit industries that fell within a given two-digit industry. This technique, which was used to construct two-digit ECIs for SICs 20, 26, 28, 29, 33, 35, 36, and 38, is shown at work in the illustration in Table C-1: a computation of an ECI at the two-digit level for SIC 28 (Chemical and Allied Products).

ECIs for the three remaining 12 international industries were calculated in a way specific to each industry. In the case of SIC 30 (Rubber and Plastic Products), there were so few interactions that an ECI was computed for only one three-digit industry, SIC 301 (Tires and Inner Tubes), and an approximate value for the entire industry was determined by counting the total number of subsidiaries in all of four three-digit indus-

---

[1] See Section II, Chapter 2.

TABLE C-1

Computation of ECIs for SIC 28

SIC Code	Total Interactions	Maximum Interactions Within		
		3 Years	5 Years	7 Years
281	193	88	114	134
282	153	73	94	114
283	178	72	98	122
284	109	53	69	76
285	25	12	14	19
287	33	15	20	27
289	60	28	38	43
Total	751	341	447	535

$$\text{Three-year ECI} = \frac{341}{751} = .454$$

$$\text{Five-year ECI} = \frac{447}{751} = .595$$

$$\text{Seven-year ECI} = \frac{535}{751} = .712$$

tries that fell within SIC 30. That is, if one U.S. parent established a subsidiary in SIC 301 and another established a subsidiary in SIC 302, this was counted as an interaction. While it is true that this procedure deviates a great deal from the usual one for computing an ECI, the three-digit and two-digit ECIs for the rubber industry are almost identical, so that it can be assumed that this type of aggregation produced no systematic bias. The two-digit value of the ECI for SIC 30 was based upon all interactions within the following three-digit industries:

SIC 301 (Tires and Inner Tubes)
SIC 302 (Rubber Footwear)
SIC 303 (Reclaimed Rubber)
SIC 306 (Fabricated Rubber Products, nec.)

SIC 32 (Stone, Clay, and Glass Products) also represented a problem of too few interactions, so that ECIs were obtainable for only two three-digit industries—SIC 321 (Flat Glass) and SIC 329 (Misc. Nonmetallic Mineral Products). Nevertheless, the glass industry so dominated SIC 32 in terms of its importance and size that its ECIs were suitable substitutes for the ECIs for SIC 32. The ECIs for the glass industry were based on all subsidiary formations in the following three-digit industries:

SIC 321 (Flat Glass)
SIC 322 (Glass and Glassware, Pressed and Blown)
SIC 323 (Products of Purchased Glass)

Finally, for SIC 37 (Transportation Equipment) it was only possible to compute ECIs at the three-digit level for SIC 371 (Motor Vehicles and Equipment) and for SIC 372 (Aircraft and Parts). But since the ECIs for SIC 372 were based on five interactions only, it was not used in any of the statistical analyses. On the other hand, the motor vehicle and equipment industry was so large that data were found that related exclusively to the U.S. and international operations of this one industry. Accordingly, in most of the analyses the ECIs and other data specific to SIC 371 were used in place of aggregated values for SIC 37.

Adjusting the eight-firm concentration ratio.—Because the procedure and the reasons for adjusting the four-firm and eight-firm concentration ratios were the same, only the eight-firm ratio enters into the following discussion on the procedure that was used.

In the publication, *Concentration Ratios in Manufacturing Industry 1963*, from which the data for this study were taken, concentration ratios are reported at the four-digit level only. In order therefore to aggregate the data to the three-digit level, it was necessary to weight the ratio for each four-digit industry by the value of the U.S. shipments of that industry; and similarly, in order to obtain weighted averages at the two-digit level, it was necessary to weight the ratios at the three-digit level by the value of U.S. shipments at the three-digit industry level.

The next step was to make simple adjustments of the two-digit industry concentration ratios in order that they might be compared with the two-digit ECIs. The ECIs for SIC 34, for example, were based on the values for SICs 341–344, 348, and 349. Likewise, the concentration ratio for SIC 34 was based on the same three-digit SICs, since the values for SICs 345–347 had been dropped from the weighting procedure. The result of these adjustments was that at the two-digit industry level, both the ECIs and the industry concentration ratios were based upon like data.

With regard once again to the concentration ratios at the four-digit industry level, there is one more reason why these data must not be used in unadjusted form. Because member firms in certain four-digit industries have taken no part whatever in the international expansion of U.S. business, if data specific to these industries had been included in the construction of the three-digit and two-digit values of the concentration ratios, this would have resulted in serious misrepresentation of the level of industry concentration at these higher levels of aggregation.

SIC 202 (Dairy Products) is a case in point. The eight-firm concentration ratio for SIC 202, calculated as the weighted average of the concentration ratios for all four-digit industries in SIC 202, was 34.9%. In view of SIC 202's relatively low concentration ratio, it is reasonable to expect that its ECIs will be low as well, but in fact its ECIs are relatively high. The reason for this is made clear when we look at the data underlying the concentration ratio in Table C-2.

The point illustrated by these data is that the eight-firm concentration ratio for SIC 202, when it is computed in this manner, is considerably lowered by SIC 2021 and SIC 2026. Thus the question that arises is whether SIC 202's concentration ratio, computed in this manner, is a good indication of the degree of concentration in segments of the dairy industry that expanded into international markets.

TABLE C-2

Value of Shipments and Eight-Firm Concentration Ratios for Four-Digit Industries in SIC 202

SIC Code	Industry Title	Value of Shipments ($ Millions)	Eight-Firm Concentration Ratio
2021	Creamery Butter	$ 989	19%
2022	Natural and Processed Cheese	1,171	51
2023	Condensed and Evaporated Milk	938	53
2024	Ice Cream and Frozen Desserts	1,076	48
2026	Fluid Milk	7,026	30

The answer, which is no, can be explained in this way. It is possible, by referring to sample data in the Multinational Enterprise Study, to identify by name those U.S. firms that set up manufacturing subsidiaries abroad in SIC 202 and, on the basis of this information, to establish that these firms manufactured and sold products in the United States in SICs 2022, 2023, and 2024. Now although it is reasonable to assume that these firms established subsidiaries overseas in the same four-digit industries, it is not paticularly reasonable to assume that they made foreign direct investments to process and sell such products as creamery butter (SIC 2021) and fluid milk (SIC 2026). Success in industries like these depends more on locational factors than on the kinds of skills these firms are likely to excel in. The point is simply this: a concentration ratio for SIC 202 that excludes data specific to those industries that are entirely domestically oriented will do a better job in the analysis than will a concentration ratio that includes all four-digit industries in SIC 202.

The problem under discussion is an example of an old and familiar problem, that is of working with data that are not at a sufficiently refined level of detail. If, for instance, the Multinational Enterprise Study had reported data on products manufactured by foreign subsidiaries at the four-digit level, the exclusion of certain four-digit industries from the computation of concentration ratios at the three-digit level would have been ɑ relatively easy matter.

Nevertheless, since it is possible to identify by name all com panies that have established manufacturing facilities in any three-digit industry, it is also possible to exclude from the com putation of the eight-firm concentration ratios those four-digi industries that have no influence on the level of concentration in industries that have been engaged in international expan sion. Such adjustments were made for a number of three-digi industries, and the details are presented in Table C-3.

TABLE C-3

Four-Digit Industries Included in the Calculation of Four-Firm and Eight-Firm Concentration Ratios for Three-Digit Industries

Three-Digit Industries	Four-Digit Industries Included in each Three-Digit Industry
202	2022–2024
203	2031–2035
205	2052
285	total value for SIC 28 (only large chemical firms with operations in all sub-industries in SIC 28 expanded into 285 overseas)
287	2879
348	3357
	(only two major firms in non-ferrous wire drawing-3357-expanded into 348 overseas)
362	3621, 3623, 3624, 3629
367	3671–3674

APPENDIX D

Industry Concentration Ratios

The stability of U.S. manufacturing industry concentration ratios.—Since the ECIs are measures of firm conduct in the years 1948–1967, the relationship that was shown to exist between the ECIs and concentration ratios is valid only if the concentration ratios for 1963 reflect industry structure for the entire twenty years. Professor Bain has this to say about the immutability of industry structure:

> The record shows that *on the average* . . . concentration within industries has changed little for quite a while; for example, one Census publication indicates that from 1935 to 1947, with respect to 103 comparably defined 4-digit manufacturing industries, concentration as measured by the 4-firm concentration ratio increased perceptibly in 33 cases, decreased perceptibly in 34 cases, and was substantially unchanged in 36 cases. Subsequent studies, carrying us to 1958 or beyond, have revealed a similar sluggishness in the average of individual-industry concentration ratios. Still, there is evidently an appreciable variance in seller concentration within many individual industries, so that we cannot assume, for purposes of statistical testing, that individual-industry concentrations are in general practically immutable for periods as long as a decade.[1]

Now let us look at evidence, beyond that cited by Bain, that concerns the stability of industry concentration. In *Concentration Ratios in Manufacturing Industry, 1963*, data can be found for 147

[1] Joe S. Bain, "The Comparative Stability of Market Structure," in Markham and Papanek (eds.), *Industrial Organization and Economic Development*, p. 44.

four-digit industries whose SIC definitions have remained essentially unchanged since 1947. (See *Census of Manufactures—1947* and *Census of Manufactures—1963*.) Intercorrelation of the eight-firm concentration ratios for the 147 industries gave the results shown in Table D-1.

TABLE D-1

**Pearson Coefficients of Intercorrelation
of Eight-Firm Concentration Ratios
for 147 Four-Digit Industries**

Concentration Ratios Based on the Census of Manufactures of:	1947	Concentration Ratios Based on the Census of Manufactures of: 1954	1958	1963
1947	1.00	.97	.94	.92
1954		1.00	.98	.95
1958			1.00	.97
1963				1.00

NOTE: All coefficients are positive and statistically significant at the .001 level.

Notice that these ratios, when considered in the aggregate, show a high degree of stability over time. Moreover, when they were grouped by two-digit industries, they showed once more a high degree of stability. Intercorrelation of the ratios within two-digit industries (the ratios fell within 13 two-digit industries) produced Pearson coefficients of $+.85$ or above; all were statistically significant at the .01 level.

Although evidence, based on samples of U.S. manufacturing, shows that industry concentration ratios have remained relatively stable during the last decade or two, so that it is reasonable to suppose that the ratios for most industries have not fluctuated widely, it may at once be admitted that 1963 concentration data are not wholly the best data. Nevertheless, reliance on such data need not necessarily have produced misleading results, since the ECIs were based on the behavior of 187 large U.S. corporations, many of which have long been dominant sellers in their industries; and it is therefore likely that changes in seller concentration in these industries would not have been as drastic as changes in other, smaller industries.

U.S. and foreign industry concentration compared.—U.S. eight-firm concentration ratios were used in the research as the indicator of industry structure. Since, however, the research was concerned with how oligopolists respond to their rivals' acts in one country and then another, one could argue that the exclusive reliance on U.S. concentration data would lead to erroneous conclusions unless the structures of industries were more or less comparable one country to the next. Although data were not available for determining concentration by industry for all 23 countries, for a few major foreign markets it was possible to determine that the patterns of industry structure were roughly the same as those in the United States.

A number of investigators have pointed out that a given industry's seller concentration ratio is much the same in the United Kingdom as in the United States, which is to say that the U.S. ratios ought to be valid proxies for their English counterparts.[2] Similarities between industry structure in the United States and in other countries are, however, less well documented, and data for deciding the issue are limited in quality and quantity. Nevertheless, by using data presented at U.S. Senate Hearings (1968) on economic concentration outside the United States, it was possible to calculate concentration ratios for 13 two-digit industries that operated in Japan, West Germany, and France.[3] Rank order correlation of the 13 industries' concentration ratios in the United States and in the three countries above gave the results shown in Table D-2.

Though the evidence is by no means conclusive, it does point out the tendency of industries to have a structure of

---

[2] See, for example, the testimony of Professor P. Sargant Florence in U.S. Senate, Subcommittee of Antitrust and Monopoly of the Committee on the Judiciary, *Economic Concentration, Part 7, Concentration Outside the United States*, 90th Cong., 2d Sess., 1968, pp. 3571–3581, and Bain, *International Differences in Industrial Structure*, p. 77.

[3] These ratios were calculated from *Economic Concentration, Part 7*, for industries corresponding to SICs 20, 22, 26, 27, 28, 29, 30, 32–37.

TABLE D-2

Spearman Coefficients of Intercorrelation of Concentration Ratios for Thirteen Two-Digit Industries in the United States, Japan, West Germany, and France
(N = 13)

	United States	Japan	West Germany	France
United States	1.00	.71	.81	.85
Japan		1.00	.72	.85
West Germany			1.00	.89
France				1.00

NOTE: All coefficients are positive and statistically significant at the .01 level.

seller concentration that is roughly the same from one industrialized country to the next.[4]

[4] For a comprehensive test of the similarity of industrial concentration in a number of leading countries see Frederic L. Pryor, "An International Comparison of Concentration Ratios," *Review of Economics and Statistics*, Vol. LIV, No. 2 (May 1972), pp. 130–140. Pryor compares the four-firm concentration ratios among a dozen large industrial countries and demonstrates that they are roughly the same.

APPENDIX E

Randomized Entry Concentration
Indexes by Industry

TABLE E-1
Three-Year ECIs for Three-Digit Industries

SIC Code	Three-Year ECIs	SIC Code	Three-Year ECIs	SIC Code	Three-Year ECIs
201	.374	291	.469	356	.478
202	.429	299	.450	357	.406
203	.450	301	.457	358	.418
204	.471	321	.481	361	.449
205	.445	329	.476	362	.415
206	.490	333	.437	363	.462
207	.467	335	.330	364	.480
208	.426	336	.435	365	.330
209	.487	341	.383	366	.374
264	.466	342	.482	367	.436
265	.449	343	.450	369	.472
281	.418	344	.400	371	.424
282	.431	348	.470	372	.426
283	.434	349	.485	381	.426
284	.463	351	.480	382	.470
285	.383	352	.473	384	.390
287	.472	353	.474	386	.540
289	.489	355	.449	399	.477

APPENDIX F

Product Tradability and Entry Concentration

The hypothesis.—The extent of oligopolistic reaction may be in part determined by the degree to which an industry's products are easily or not easily transported between markets. When, for instance, products are highly tradable—the cost and difficulties involved in supplying country A from countries B or C are minimal—then the establishment of a production facility in country A by one member of an industry may be viewed as a minor threat by other members of the industry with manufacturing plants in countries B or C. Thus in industries where the logistics of supplying foreign markets are relatively uncomplicated and inexpensive, and where the options of sourcing are multiple, one would not expect to find a high level of oligopolistic reaction.

The product tradability index.—Testing the hypothesis calls for a statistic that measures the extent to which U.S. firms have the option of transshipping products among markets from manufacturing sites located in the United States and in foreign countries. Data limitations required the use of a measure, the product tradability index, that reflects, albeit crudely, the ability of U.S. industries to supply markets from multiple sources.[1] For each of the 12 international two-digit industries

---

[1] The concept of the product tradability index was borrowed from Lawrence Franko, "Strategy Choice and Multinational Corporate Tolerance for Joint Ventures with Foreign Partners."

the product tradability index is the sum of the dollar values of its 1963 U.S. exports and imports divided by the total value of its 1963 U.S. production.

TABLE F-1

Product Tradability Indexes

SIC Code	Industry Title	Index
20	Food and Kindred Products	.058
26	Paper and Allied Products	.097
28	Chemicals and Allied Products	.083
29	Petroleum and Coal Products	.073
30	Rubber and Plastics Products	.039
32	Stone, Clay, and Glass Products	.040
33	Primary Metal Industries	.072
34	Fabricated Metal Products	.035
35	Machinery, Except Electrical	.145
36	Electrical Equipment and Supplies	.063
37	Transportation Equipment	.064
38	Instruments and Related Products	.133

SOURCE: Bureau of the Census, *U.S. Commodity Exports and Imports as Related to Output, 1966 and 1965* and *Census of Manufactures, 1963*.

Pearson and rank correlation of the product tradability indexes with the corresponding ECIs gave negative coefficients, but in all cases the level of statistical significance was unacceptable. Inspection of the data disclosed that the ECIs for SIC 30 were abnormally low in light of the low value of the product tradability index for the industry. We have seen (Chapters 3 and 4) that the relationship of the ECIs for SIC 30 with other variables does not seem to follow the pattern set by other industries, largely, it appears, because of absence of new entrants into the rubber industry.

The correlations between the product tradability indexes and the ECIs were rerun for 11 two-digit industries, excluding SIC 30, resulting in an improvement in the level of statistical significance of all coefficients. Typical of the results was the

Pearson coefficient of correlation of the average ECIs with the product tradability indexes: $-.53$ (.047).

If it is accepted that the product tradability index, measuring as it does the extent to which products by industry have flowed in U.S. international trade relative to U.S. production of the same products, reflects the ability of various U.S. industries to transship products among markets, then there seems to be no reason to reject the hypothesis. Furthermore, the finding is consistent with the general concept illustrated by many of the other findings in this study: that is, the intensity of oligopolistic reaction is determined by the number and the nature of options open to firms to ignore the moves of near rivals.

BIBLIOGRAPHY

Articles

Balassa, Bela. "American Direct Investments in the Common Market," *Banca Nazionale del Lavoro Quarterly Review*, No. 77 (June 1966), pp. 121–146.

Comanor, William S., and Thomas A. Wilson. "Advertising Market Structure and Performance," *Review of Economics and Statistics*, Vol. XLIV, No. 4 (November 1967), pp. 423–440.

————. "Theory of the Firm and of Market Structure: Advertising and the Advantage of Size," *American Economic Review*, Vol. XLIV, No. 2 (May 1969), pp. 87–98.

Grossack, Irvin M. "Towards an Integration of Static and Dynamic Measures of Industry Concentration," *Review of Economics and Statistics*, Vol. XLVII, No. 3 (August 1965), pp. 301–308.

Gruber, William, Dileep Mehta, and Raymond Vernon. "The R&D Factor in International Trade and International Investment of United States Industries," *Journal of Political Economy*, Vol. LXXV, No. 1 (February 1967), pp. 20–35. (Reprinted in Louis T. Wells, Jr. (ed.). *The Product Life Cycle and International Trade.* Boston: Division of Research, Harvard Business School, 1972.)

Hammond, John S., III. "Better Decisions with Preference Theory," *Harvard Business Review*, Vol. 49, No. 6 (November–December 1967), pp. 123–141.

Houthakker, H. S., and Stephen P. Magee. "Income and Price Elasticities in World Trade," *Review of Economics and Statistics*, Vol. LI, No. 2 (May 1969), pp. 111–123.

Hymer, Stephen. "The Efficiency (Contradictions) of Multinational

Corporations," *American Economic Review*, Vol. LX, No. 2 (May 1970), pp. 441–448.

Mann, H. Michael. "Asymmetry, Barriers to Entry and Rates of Return in Twenty-Six Concentrated Industries, 1948 to 1957," *Western Economic Journal*, Vol. VIII, No. 1 (March 1970), pp. 86–89.

Mann, H. M., J. A. Henning, and J. W. Meehan, Jr. "Advertising and Concentration: An Empirical Investigation," *Journal of Industrial Economics*, Vol. XVI, No. 1 (November 1967), pp. 34–45.

Markham, Jesse W. "Market Structure, Business Conduct, and Innovation," *American Economic Review*, Vol. LV, No. 2 (May 1965), pp. 323–332.

————. "Oligopoly," in David L. Sills (ed.), *International Encyclopedia of the Social Sciences*, Vol. XI (1968), pp. 283–290.

Miller, Richard A. "Market Structure and Industrial Performance: Relation of Profit Rates to Concentration, Advertising Intensity, and Diversity," *Journal of Industrial Economics*, Vol. XVII, No. 2 (April 1969), pp. 104–118.

Pryor, Frederic L. "An International Comparison of Concentration Ratios," *Review of Economics and Statistics*, Vol. LIV, No. 2 (May 1972), pp. 130–140.

Scaperlanda, Anthony E., and Lawrence J. Mauer. "The Determinants of U.S. Direct Investment in the E.E.C.," *American Economic Review*, Vol. LIX, No. 4, Part 1 (September 1969), pp. 558–568.

Scherer, Frederic M. "Corporate Inventive Output, Profits, and Growth," *Journal of Political Economy*, Vol. LXXIII, No. 3 (June 1965), pp. 290–297.

————. "Firm Size, Market Structure, Opportunity, and the Output of Patented Inventions," *American Economic Review*, Vol. LV, No. 5, Part 1 (December 1965), pp. 1097–1123.

————. "Market Structure and the Employment of Scientists and Engineers," *American Economic Review*, Vol. LVII, No. 3 (June 1967), pp. 524–531.

————. "Market Structure and the Stability of Investment,"

American Economic Review, Vol. XLIX, No. 2 (May 1969), pp. 72–79.

Telser, L. G. "Advertising and Competition," *Journal of Political Economy*, Vol. 72, No. 6 (December 1964), pp. 537–562.

————. "Another Look at Advertising and Concentration," *Journal of Industrial Economics*, Vol. XVIII, No. 1 (November 1969), pp. 85–94.

Vernon, Raymond. "Conflict and Resolution Between Foreign Direct Investors and Less Developed Countries," *Public Policy*, Vol. XVII (Fall 1968), pp. 333–351.

————. "International Investment and International Trade in the Product Cycle," *Quarterly Journal of Economics*, Vol. LXXX, No. 2 (May 1966), pp. 190–207.

Williamson, Oliver. "A Dynamic Theory of Interfirm Behavior," *Quarterly Journal of Economics*, Vol. LXXIX, No. 4 (November 1965), pp. 579–607.

Books

Aharoni, Yair. *The Foreign Investment Decision Process.* Boston: Division of Research, Harvard Business School, 1966.

Bain, Joe S. *Industrial Organization.* New York: John Wiley and Sons, Inc., 2d ed., 1968.

————. *International Differences in Industrial Structure.* New Haven: Yale University Press, 1966.

Baumol, William J. *Business Behavior, Value, and Growth.* New York: Harcourt, Brace & World, Inc., rev., 1967.

Behrman, Jack N. *Some Patterns in the Rise of the Multinational Enterprise.* Chapel Hill: University of North Carolina, Research Paper 18, 1969.

Bower, Joseph L. *Managing the Resource Allocation Process: A Study of Corporate Planning and Investment.* Boston: Division of Research, Harvard Business School, 1970.

Brash, Donald T. *American Investment in Australian Industry.* Cambridge: Harvard University Press, 1966.

Caves, Richard E. *American Industry: Structure, Conduct, Performance.* Englewood Cliffs: Prentice-Hall, Inc., 2d ed., 1967.

Chamberlin, E. H. *The Theory of Monopolistic Competition.* Cambridge: Harvard University Press, 8th ed., 1962.

Chandler, A. D., Jr. *Strategy and Structure.* Cambridge: The M.I.T. Press, 1962.

Cyert, Richard M., and James G. March. *A Behavioral Theory of the Firm.* Englewood Cliffs: Prentice-Hall, Inc., 1963.

Dunning, John H. *American Investment in British Manufacturing Industry.* London: George Allen and Unwin Ltd., 1958.

————. *The Role of American Investment in the British Economy.* London: P.E.P., 1969.

Gort, Michael. *Diversification and Integration in American Industry.* Princeton: Princeton University Press, 1962.

Kaysen, Carl, and Donald T. Turner. *Antitrust Policy.* Cambridge: Harvard University Press, 1959.

Kindleberger, Charles P. *American Business Abroad.* New Haven: Yale University Press, 1969.

———— (ed.). *The International Corporation.* Cambridge: The M.I.T. Press, 1970.

Kuenne, R. E. (ed.). *Monopolistic Competition Theory: Essays in Honor of Edward H. Chamberlin.* New York: John Wiley and Sons, Inc., 1967.

Markham, J. W., and G. F. Papanek (eds.). *Industrial Organization and Economic Development.* Boston: Houghton Mifflin Company, 1970.

Mason, Edward S. *Economic Concentration and the Monopoly Problem.* Cambridge: Harvard University Press, 1959.

von Neumann, J., and O. Morgenstern. *The Theory of Games and Economic Behavior.* Princeton: Princeton University Press, 3d ed., 1953.

Polk, Judd, Irene Meister, and Lawrence A. Veit. *U.S. Production Abroad and the Balance of Payments.* New York: National Industrial Conference Board, 1966.

Richardson, G. B. *Information and Investment.* London: Oxford University Press, 1960.

Robinson, Harry J. *The Motivation and Flow of Private Foreign Investment.* Menlo Park: Stanford Research Institute, 1961.

Robinson, Joan. *The Economics of Imperfect Competition.* London: Macmillan and Co. Ltd., 2d ed., 1969.

Safarian, E. A. *Foreign Ownership of Canadian Industry.* New York: McGraw-Hill Book Company, 1960.

Schelling, Thomas C. *The Strategy of Conflict.* London: Oxford University Press, 1960.

Shubik, Martin. *Strategy and Market Structure.* New York: John Wiley and Sons, Inc., 1959.

Stopford, John M., and Louis T. Wells, Jr. *Managing the Multinational Enterprise: Organization of the Firm and Ownership of the Subsidiaries.* New York: Basic Books, Inc., 1972.

Vaupel, James W., and Joan P. Curhan. *The Making of Multinational Enterprise.* Boston: Division of Research, Harvard Business School, 1971.

Vernon, Raymond. *Manager in the International Economy.* Englewood Cliffs: Prentice-Hall, Inc., 1968.

———. *Sovereignty at Bay: The Multinational Spread of U.S. Enterprises.* New York: Basic Books, Inc., 1971.

Government Publications

Arnould, Richard J. *Diversification and Profitability Among Large Food Processing Firms.* U.S. Department of Agriculture, Economic Report No. 171. Washington: Government Printing Office, 1970.

Bureau of Economics, Federal Trade Commission. *Economic Papers, 1966–1969.* Washington: Government Printing Office, 1970.

Internal Revenue Service. *Corporation Income Tax Returns: With Accounting Periods Ended July 1960–June 1961.* Washington: Government Printing Office, 1963.

———. *Statistics of Income, 1962: Foreign Income and Taxes Reported on Corporation Income Tax Returns.* Washington: Government Printing Office, 1969.

National Science Foundation. *Research and Development in Industry, 1967.* Washington: Government Printing Office, 1969.

U.S. Senate, Subcommittee on Antitrust and Monopoly of the Committee on the Judiciary. *Concentration Ratios in Manufacturing Industry, 1963.* 89th Cong., 2d Sess., 1966.

——————. *Hearings, Economic Concentration, Part 3, Concentration, Invention, and Innovation.* 89th Cong., 1st Sess., 1965.

——————. *Hearings, Economic Concentration, Part 7, Concentration Outside the United States.* 90th Cong., 2d Sess., 1968.

Unpublished Material

Franko, Lawrence. "Strategy Choice and Multinational Corporate Tolerance for Joint Ventures with Foreign Partners." Unpublished doctoral dissertation, Harvard Business School, 1969.

Hymer, Stephen. "The International Operations of National Firms —A Study of Direct Foreign Investment." Unpublished doctoral dissertation, Massachusetts Institute of Technology, 1960.

Stobaugh, Robert B., Jr. "The Product Life Cycle, U.S. Exports, and International Investment." Unpublished doctoral dissertation, Harvard Business School, 1968.

Stopford, John M. "Growth and Organizational Change in the Multinational Firm." Unpublished doctoral dissertation, Harvard Business School, 1968.

INDEX